ABOUT LOOKING

ABOUT LOOKING

JOHN BERGER

With 26 Illustrations

Pantheon Books, New York

AR
701. 15
B4 96

LIBRARY OF CONGRESS CATALOGING IN PUBLICATION DATA
Berger, John.
  About looking.

  1. Art—Psychology. 2. Visual perception.
3. Meaning (Psychology) I. Title.
N71.B398   701'.1'5   79-3615
ISBN 0-394-51124-7
ISBN 0-394-73907-8 pbk.

Picture acknowledgements in back of book
Designed by Chris Hyde

Manufactured in the United States of America
FIRST AMERICAN EDITION

To Anthony Barnett, who is always looking.

Contents

Acknowledgements

All the articles in this book appeared in their original form in *New Society* with the exception of the following: ''Between Two Colmars'' and ''Romaine Lorquet'', which first appeared in *The Guardian*; and ''Turner and the Barber's Shop'' and ''Rouault and the Suburbs of Paris'', which first appeared in *Realities* (Paris). Of these articles, the ones on Lowry, Hals, Rodin and Giacometti appeared in *The Moment of Cubism and other essays*, which is now unobtainable.

I would like to thank the Transnational Institute, Amsterdam, for their encouragement and support during the time when many of these essays and articles were written. And I would like to express my continuing solidarity with this Institute.

WHY LOOK AT ANIMALS?

Why Look at Animals?

For Gilles Aillaud

The 19th century, in western Europe and North America, saw the beginning of a process, today being completed by 20th century corporate capitalism, by which every tradition which has previously mediated between man and nature was broken. Before this rupture, animals constituted the first circle of what surrounded man. Perhaps that already suggests too great a distance. They were with man at the centre of his world. Such centrality was of course economic and productive. Whatever the changes in productive means and

1

social organisation, men depended upon animals for food, work, transport, clothing.

Yet to suppose that animals first entered the human imagination as meat or leather or horn is to project a 19th century attitude backwards across the millenia. Animals first entered the imagination as messengers and promises. For example, the domestication of cattle did not begin as a simple prospect of milk and meat. Cattle had magical functions, sometimes oracular, sometimes sacrificial. And the choice of a given species as magical, tameable *and* alimentary was originally determined by the habits, proximity and "invitation" of the animal in question.

> White ox good is my mother
> And we the people of my sister,
> The people of Nyariau Bul . . .
> Friend, great ox of the spreading horns,
> which ever bellows amid the herd,
> Ox of the son of Bul Maloa.

(The Nuer: a description of the modes of livelihood and political institutions of a Nilotic people, by Evans-Pritchard.)

Animals are born, are sentient and are mortal. In these things they resemble man. In their superficial anatomy — less in their deep anatomy — in their habits, in their time, in their physical capacities, they differ from man. They are both like and unlike.

"We know what animals do and what beaver and bears and salmon and other creatures need, because once our men were married to them and they acquired this knowledge from their animal wives." (Hawaiian Indians quoted by Lévi-Strauss in *The Savage Mind*.)

The eyes of an animal when they consider a man are attentive and wary. The same animal may well look at other

2

species in the same way. He does not reserve a special look for man. But by no other species except man will the animal's look be recognised as familiar. Other animals are held by the look. Man becomes aware of himself returning the look.

The animal scrutinises him across a narrow abyss of non-comprehension. This is why the man can surprise the animal. Yet the animal — even if domesticated — can also surprise the man. The man too is looking across a similar, but not identical, abyss of non-comprehension. And this is so wherever he looks. He is always looking across ignorance and fear. And so, when he is *being seen* by the animal, he is being seen as his surroundings are seen by him. His recognition of this is what makes the look of the animal familiar. And yet the animal is distinct, and can never be confused with man. Thus, a power is ascribed to the animal, comparable with human power but never coinciding with it. The animal has secrets which, unlike the secrets of caves, mountains, seas, are specifically addressed to man.

The relation may become clearer by comparing the look of an animal with the look of another man. Between two men the two abysses are, in principle, bridged by language. Even if the encounter is hostile and no words are used (even if the two speak different languages), the *existence* of language allows that at least one of them, if not both mutually, is confirmed by the other. Language allows men to reckon with each other as with themselves. (In the confirmation made possible by language, human ignorance and fear may also be confirmed. Whereas in animals fear is a response to signal, in men it is endemic.)

No animal confirms man, either positively or negatively. The animal can be killed and eaten so that its energy is added to that which the hunter already possesses. The animal

3

can be tamed so that it supplies and works for the peasant. But always its lack of common language, its silence, guarantees its distance, its distinctness, its exclusion, from and of man.

Just because of this distinctness, however, an animal's life, never to be confused with a man's, can be seen to run parallel to his. Only in death do the two parallel lines converge and after death, perhaps, cross over to become parallel again: hence the widespread belief in the transmigration of souls.

With their parallel lives, animals offer man a companionship which is different from any offered by human exchange. Different because it is a companionship offered to the loneliness of man as a species.

Such an unspeaking companionship was felt to be so equal that often one finds the conviction that it was man who lacked the capacity to speak with animals — 'hence the stories and legends of exceptional beings, like Orpheus, who could talk with animals in their own language.

What were the secrets of the animal's likeness with, and unlikeness from man? The secrets whose existence man recognised as soon as he intercepted an animal's look.

In one sense the whole of anthropology, concerned with the passage from nature to culture, is an answer to that question. But there is also a general answer. All the secrets were about animals as an *intercession* between man and his origin. Darwin's evolutionary theory, indelibly stamped as it is with the marks of the European 19th century, nevertheless belongs to a tradition, almost as old as man himself. Animals interceded between man and their origin because they were both like and unlike man.

Animals came from over the horizon. They belonged *there* and *here*. Likewise they were mortal and immortal. An animal's blood flowed like human blood, but its species was undying and each lion was Lion, each ox was Ox. This — maybe the first existential dualism — was reflected in the treatment of animals. They were subjected *and* worshipped, bred *and* sacrificed.

Today the vestiges of this dualism remain among those who live intimately with, and depend upon, animals. A peasant becomes fond of his pig and is glad to salt away its pork. What is significant, and is so difficult for the urban stranger to understand, is that the two statements in that sentence are connected by an *and* and not by a *but*.

The parallelism of their similar/dissimilar lives allowed animals to provoke some of the first questions and offer answers. The first subject matter for painting was animal. Probably the first paint was animal blood. Prior to that, it is not unreasonable to suppose that the first metaphor was animal. Rousseau, in his *Essay on the Origins of Languages,* maintained that language itself began with metaphor: "As emotions were the first motives which induced man to speak, his first utterances were tropes (metaphors). Figurative language was the first to be born, proper meanings were the last to be found."

If the first metaphor was animal, it was because the essential relation between man and animal was metaphoric. Within that relation what the two terms — man and animal — shared in common revealed what differentiated them. And vice versa.

In his book on totemism, Lévi-Strauss comments on Rousseau's reasoning: "It is because man originally felt himself identical to all those like him (among which, as Rousseau explicitly says, we must include animals) that he came to acquire the capacity to distinguish *himself* as he distinguishes *them* — ie, to use the diversity of species for conceptual support for social differentiation."

To accept Rousseau's explanation of the origins of language is, of course, to beg certain questions (what was the minimal social organisation necessary for the break-through of language?). Yet no search for origin can ever be fully satisfied. The intercession of animals in that search was so common precisely because animals remain ambiguous.

All theories of ultimate origin are only ways of better defining what followed. Those who disagree with Rousseau are contesting a view of man, not a historical fact. What we are trying to define, because the experience is almost lost, is the universal use of animal-signs for charting the experience of the world.

Animals were seen in eight out of twelve signs of the zodiac. Among the Greeks, the sign of each of the twelve hours of the day was an animal. (The first a cat, the last a crocodile.) The Hindus envisaged the earth being carried on the back of an elephant and the elephant on a tortoise. For the Nuer of the southern Sudan (see Roy Willis's *Man and Beast*), "all creatures, including man, originally lived together in fellowship in one camp. Dissension began after Fox persuaded Mongoose to throw a club into Elephant's face. A quarrel ensued and the animals separated; each went its own way and began to live as they now are, and to kill each other. Stomach, which at first lived a life of its own in the bush, entered into man so that now he is always hungry. The sexual organs, which had also been separate, attached themselves to men and women, causing them to desire one another constantly. Elephant taught man how to pound millet so that now he satisfies his hunger only by ceaseless labour. Mouse taught man to beget and women to bear. And Dog brought fire to man."

The examples are endless. Everywhere animals offered explanations, or more precisely, lent their name or character to a quality, which like all qualities, was, in its essence, mysterious.

What distinguished man from animals was the human capacity for symbolic thought, the capacity which was inseparable from the development of language in which words were not mere signals, but signifiers of something other than themselves. Yet the first symbols were animals. What distinguished men from animals was born of their relationship with them.

The *Iliad* is one of the earliest texts available to us, and in it the use of metaphor still reveals the proximity of man and animal, the proximity from which metaphor itself arose. Homer describes the death of a soldier on the battlefield and then the death of a horse. Both deaths are equally transparent to Homer's eyes, there is no more refraction in one case than the other.

"Meanwhile, Idomeneus struck Erymas on the mouth with his relentless bronze. The metal point of the spear passed right through the lower part of his skull, under the brain and smashed the white bones. His teeth were shattered; both his eyes were filled with blood; and he spurted blood through his nostrils and his gaping mouth. Then the black cloud of Death descended on him." That was a man.

Three pages further on, it is a horse who falls: "Sarpedon, casting second with his shining spear, missed Patroclus but struck his horse Pedasus on the right shoulder. The horse whinnied in the throes of Death, then fell down in the dust and with a great sigh gave up his life." That was animal.

Book 17 of the *Iliad* opens with Menelaus standing over the corpse of Patroclus to prevent the Trojans stripping it. Here Homer uses animals as metaphoric references, to convey, with irony or admiration, the excessive or superlative qualities of different moments. *Without the example of animals,* such moments would have remained indescribable. "Menelaus bestrode his body like a fretful mother cow standing over the first calf she has brought into the world."

A Trojan threatens him, and ironically Menelaus shouts out to Zeus: "Have you ever seen such arrogance? We know the courage of the panther and the lion and the fierce wild-boar, the most high-spirited and self-reliant beast of all, but that, it seems, is nothing to the prowess of these sons of Panthous . . .!"

Menelaus then kills the Trojan who threatened him, and nobody dares approach him. "He was like a mountain lion who believes in his own strength and pounces on the finest heifer in a grazing herd. He breaks her neck with his powerful jaws, and then he tears her to pieces and devours her blood and entrails, while all around him the herdsmen and their dogs create a din but keep their distance — they are heartily scared of him and nothing would induce them to close in."

Centuries after Homer, Aristotle, in his *History of Animals,* the first major scientific work on the subject, systematises the comparative relation of man and animal.

"In the great majority of animals there are traces of physical qualities and attitudes, which qualities are more markedly differentiated in the case of human beings. For just as we pointed out resemblances in the physical organs, so in a number of animals we observe gentleness and fierceness, mildness or cross-temper, courage or timidity, fear or confidence, high spirits or low cunning, and, with regard to intelligence, something akin to sagacity. Some of these qualities in man, as compared with the corresponding qualities in animals, differ only quantitatively: that is to say, man has more or less of this quality, and an animal has more or less of some other; other qualities in man are represented by analogous and not identical qualities; for example, just as in man we find knowledge, wisdom and sagacity, so in certain animals there exists some other natural potentiality akin to these. The truth of this statement will be the more clearly apprehended if we have regard to the phenomena of childhood: for in children we observe the traces and seeds of what will one day be settled psychological habits, though psychologically a child hardly differs for the time being from an animal . . .''

To most modern ''educated'' readers, this passage, I think, will seem noble but too anthropomorphic. Gentleness, cross-temper, sagacity, they would argue, are not moral qualities which can be ascribed to animals. And the behaviourists would support this objection.

Until the 19th century, however, anthropomorphism was integral to the relation between man and animal and was an expression of their proximity. Anthropomorphism was the residue of the continuous use of animal metaphor. In the last two centuries, animals have gradually disappeared. Today we live without them. And in this new solitude, anthropomorphism makes us doubly uneasy.

The decisive theoretical break came with Descartes. Descartes internalised, *within man,* the dualism implicit in the human relation to animals. In dividing absolutely body from soul, he bequeathed the body to the laws of physics and mechanics, and, since animals were soulless, the animal was reduced to the model of a machine.

The consequences of Descartes's break followed only slowly. A century later, the great zoologist Buffon, although accepting and using the model of the machine in order to classify animals and their capacities, nevertheless displays a tenderness towards animals which temporarily reinstates them as companions. This tenderness is half envious.

9

What man has to do in order to transcend the animal, to transcend the mechanical within himself, and what his unique spirituality leads to, is often anguish. And so, by comparison and despite the model of the machine, the animal seems to him to enjoy a kind of innocence. The animal has been emptied of experience and secrets, and this new invented ''innocence'' begins to provoke in man a kind of nostalgia. For the first time, animals are placed in a *receding* past. Buffon, writing on the beaver, says this:

''To the same degree as man has raised himself above the state of nature, animals have fallen below it: conquered and turned into slaves, or treated as rebels and scattered by force, their societies have faded away, their industry has become unproductive, their tentative arts have disappeared; each species has lost its general qualities, all of them retaining only their distinct capacities, developed in some by example, imitation, education, and in others, by fear and necessity during the constant watch for survival. What visions and plans can these soulless slaves have, these relics of the past without power?

''Only vestiges of their once marvellous industry remain in far deserted places, unknown to man for centuries, where each species freely used its natural capacities and perfected them in peace within a lasting community. The beavers are perhaps the only remaining example, the last monument to that animal intelligence . . .''

Although such nostalgia towards animals was an 18th century invention, countless *productive* inventions were still necessary — the railway, electricity, the conveyor belt, the canning industry, the motor car, chemical fertilisers — before animals could be marginalised.

During the 20th century, the internal combustion engine displaced draught animals in streets and factories. Cities,

growing at an ever increasing rate, transformed the surrounding countryside into suburbs where field animals, wild or
domesticated, became rare. The commercial exploitation of
certain species (bison, tigers, reindeer) has rendered them
almost extinct. Such wild life as remains is increasingly confined to national parks and game reserves.

Eventually, Descartes's model was surpassed. In the first
stages of the industrial revolution, animals were used as
machines. As also were children. Later, in the so-called
post-industrial societies, they are treated as raw material.
Animals required for food are processed like manufactured
commodities.

"Another giant [plant], now under development in North
Carolina, will cover a total of 150,000 hectares but will
employ only 1,000 people, one for every 15 hectares. Grains
will be sown, nurtured and harvested by machines, including airplanes. They will be fed to the 50,000 cattle and
hogs . . . those animals will never touch the ground. They
will be bred, suckled and fed to maturity in specially designed pens." (Susan George's *How the Other Half Dies*.)

This reduction of the animal, which has a theoretical as
well as economic history, is part of the same process as that
by which men have been reduced to isolated productive and
consuming units. Indeed, during this period an approach to
animals often prefigured an approach to man. The
mechanical view of the animal's work capacity was later
applied to that of workers. F. W. Taylor who developed the
"Taylorism" of time-motion studies and "scientific"
management of industry proposed that work must be "so
stupid" and so phlegmatic that he (the worker) "more nearly resembles in his mental make-up the ox than any other
type." Nearly all modern techniques of social conditioning
were first established with animal experiments. As were also

11

the methods of so-called intelligence testing. Today behaviourists like Skinner imprison the very concept of man within the limits of what they conclude from their artificial tests with animals.

Is there not one way in which animals, instead of disappearing, continue to multiply? Never have there been so many household pets as are to be found today in the cities of the richest countries. In the United States, it is estimated that there are at least forty million dogs, forty million cats, fifteen million cage birds and ten million other pets.

In the past, families of all classes kept domestic animals because they served a useful purpose — guard dogs, hunting dogs, mice-killing cats, and so on. The practice of keeping animals regardless of their usefulness, the keeping, exactly, of *pets* (in the 16th century the word usually referred to a lamb raised by hand) is a modern innovation, and, on the social scale on which it exists today, is unique. It is part of that universal but personal withdrawal into the private small family unit, decorated or furnished with mementoes from the outside world, which is such a distinguishing feature of consumer societies.

The small family living unit lacks space, earth, other animals, seasons, natural temperatures, and so on. The pet is either sterilised or sexually isolated, extremely limited in its exercise, deprived of almost all other animal contact, and fed with artificial foods. This is the material process which lies behind the truism that pets come to resemble their masters or mistresses. They are creatures of their owner's way of life.

Equally important is the way the average owner regards his pet. (Children are, briefly, somewhat different.) The pet *completes* him, offering responses to aspects of his character which would otherwise remain unconfirmed. He can be to his pet what he is not to anybody or anything else. Further-more, the pet can be conditioned to react as though it, too, recognises this. The pet offers its owner a mirror to a part that is otherwise never reflected. But, since in this relation-ship the autonomy of both parties has been lost (the owner has become the-special-man-he-is-only-to-his-pet, and the animal has become dependent on its owner for every physical need), the parallelism of their separate lives has been destroyed.

The cultural marginalisation of animals is, of course, a more complex process than their physical marginalisation. The animals of the mind cannot be so easily dispersed. Say-ings, dreams, games, stories, superstitions, the language itself, recall them. The animals of the mind, instead of being dispersed, have been co-opted into other categories so that the category *animal* has lost its central importance. Mostly they have been co-opted into the *family* and into the *spectacle*.

Those co-opted into the family somewhat resemble pets. But having no physical needs or limitations as pets do, they can be totally transformed into human puppets. The books and drawings of Beatrix Potter are an early example; all the animal productions of the Disney industry are a more recent and extreme one. In such works the pettiness of current social practices is *universalised* by being projected on to the animal kingdom. The following dialogue between Donald Duck and his nephews is eloquent enough.

"DONALD: Man, what a day! What a perfect day for fishing, boating, dating or picnicking — only I can't do *any* of these things!

NEPHEW: Why not, Unca Donald? What's holding you back?

DONALD: The Bread of Life boys! As usual, I'm broke and its eons till payday.

NEPHEW: You could take a walk Unca Donald — go bird-watching.
DONALD: (groan!) I may *have to*! But first, I'll wait for the mailman. He may bring something good newswise!
NEPHEW: Like a cheque from an unknown relative in Moneyville?''

Their physical features apart, these animals have been absorbed into the so-called silent majority.

The animals transformed into spectacle have disappeared in another way. In the windows of bookshops at Christmas, a third of the volumes on display are animal picture books. Baby owls or giraffes, the camera fixes them in a domain which, although entirely visible to the camera, will never be entered by the spectator. All animals appear like fish seen through the plate glass of an aquarium. The reasons for this are both technical and ideological: Technically the devices used to obtain ever more arresting images — hidden cameras, telescopic lenses, flashlights, remote controls and so on — combine to produce pictures which carry with them numerous indications of their normal *invisibility*. The images exist thanks only to the existence of a technical clairvoyance.

A recent, very well-produced book of animal photographs (*La Fête Sauvage* by Frédéric Rossif) announces in its preface: "Each of these pictures lasted in real time less than three hundredths of a second, they are far beyond the capacity of the human eye. What we see here is something never before seen, because it is totally invisible."

In the accompanying ideology, animals are always the observed. The fact that they can observe us has lost all significance. They are the objects of our ever-extending knowledge. What we know about them is an index of our power, and thus an index of what separates us from them. The more we know, the further away they are.

Yet in the same ideology, as Lukacs points out in *History and Class Consciousness,* nature is also a value concept. A value opposed to the social institutions which strip man of his natural essence and imprison him. "Nature thereby acquires the meaning of what has grown organically, what was not created by man, in contrast to the artificial structures of human civilisation. At the same time, it can be understood as that aspect of human inwardness which has remained natural, or at least tends or longs to become natural once more." According to this view of nature, the life of a wild animal becomes an ideal, an ideal internalised as a feeling surrounding a repressed desire. The image of a wild animal becomes the starting-point of a daydream: a point from which the day-dreamer departs with his back turned.

The degree of confusion involved is illustrated by the following news story: "London housewife Barbara Carter won a 'grant a wish' charity contest, and said she wanted to kiss and cuddle a lion. Wednesday night she was in a hospital in shock and with throat wounds. Mrs Carter, 46, was taken to the lions' compound of the safari park at Bewdley, Wednesday. As she bent forward to stroke the lioness, Suki, it pounced and dragged her to the ground. Wardens later said. 'We seem to have made a bad error of judgment. We have always regarded the lioness as perfectly safe'."

The treatment of animals in 19th century romantic painting was already an acknowledgement of their impending disappearance. The images are of animals *receding* into a wildness that existed only in the imagination. There was, however, one 19th century artist, who was obsessed by the transformation about to take place, and whose work was an uncanny illustration òf it. Grandville published his *Public and Private Life of Animals* in instalments between 1840 and 1842.

15

At first sight, Grandville's animals, dressed up and performing as men and women, appear to belong to the old tradition, whereby a person is portrayed as an animal so as to reveal more clearly an aspect of his or her character. The device was like putting on a mask, but its function was to unmask. The animal represents the apogee of the character trait in question: the lion, absolute courage: the hare, lechery. The animal once lived near the origin of the quality. It was through the animal that the quality first became recognisable. And so the animal lends it his name.

16

But as one goes on looking at Grandville's engravings, one becomes aware that the shock which they convey derives, in fact, from the opposite movement to that which one first assumed. These animals are not being "borrowed" to explain people, nothing is being unmasked; on the contrary. These animals have become prisoners of a human/social situation into which they have been press-ganged. The vulture as landlord is more dreadfully rapacious than he is as a bird. The crocodiles at dinner are greedier at the table than they are in the river.

Here animals are not being used as reminders of origin, or as moral metaphors, they are being used *en masse* to "people" situations. The movement that ends with the banality of Disney, began as a disturbing, prophetic dream in the work of Grandville.

The dogs in Grandville's engraving of the dog-pound are in no way canine; they have dogs faces, but what they are suffering is imprisonment *like men*.

The bear is a good father shows a bear dejectedly pulling a pram like any other human bread-winner. Grandville's first volume ends with the words "Goodnight then, dear reader. Go home, lock your cage well, sleep tight and have pleasant dreams. Until tomorrow." Animals and populace are becoming synonymous, which is to say the animals are fading away.

A later Grandville drawing, entitled *The animals entering the steam ark,* is explicit. In the Judaeo-Christian tradition, Noah's Ark was the first ordered assembly of animals and man. The assembly is now over. Grandville shows us the great departure. On a quayside a long queue of different species is filing slowly away, their backs towards us. Their postures suggest all the last minute doubts of emigrants. In the distance is a ramp by which the first have already

17

entered the 19th century ark, which is like an American steamboat. The bear. The lion. The donkey. The camel. The cock. The fox. Exeunt.

"About 1867," according to the *London Zoo Guide,* "a music hall artist called the Great Vance sang a song called *Walking in the zoo is the OK thing to do,* and the word 'zoo' came into everyday use. London Zoo also brought the word 'Jumbo' into the English language. Jumbo was an African elephant of mammoth size, who lived at the zoo between 1865 and 1882. Queen Victoria took an interest in him and eventually he ended his days as the star of the famous Barnum circus which travelled through America — his name living on to describe things of giant proportions.''

Public zoos came into existence at the beginning of the period which was to see the disappearance of animals from daily life. The zoo to which people go to meet animals, to observe them, to see them, is, in fact, a monument to the impossibility of such encounters. Modern zoos are an epitaph to a relationship which was as old as man. They are not seen as such because the wrong questions have been addressed to zoos.

When they were founded — the London Zoo in 1828, the Jardin des Plantes in 1793, the Berlin Zoo in 1844, they brought considerable prestige to the national capitals. The prestige was not so different from that which had accrued to the private royal menageries. These menageries, along with gold plate, architecture, orchestras, players, furnishings, dwarfs, acrobats, uniforms, horses, art and food, had been demonstrations of an emperor's or king's power and wealth. Likewise in the 19th century, public zoos were an endorsement of modern colonial power. The capturing of the animals was a symbolic representation of the conquest of all distant and exotic lands. ''Explorers'' proved their patriotism by sending home a tiger or an elephant. The gift of an exotic animal to the metropolitan zoo became a token in subservient diplomatic relations.

Yet, like every other 19th century public institution, the zoo, however supportive of the ideology of imperialism, had to claim an independent and civic function. The claim was that it was another kind of museum, whose purpose was to further knowledge and public enlightenment. And so the first questions asked of zoos belonged to natural history; it was then thought possible to study the natural life of animals even in such unnatural conditions. A century later, more sophisticated zoologists such as Konrad Lorenz asked behaviouristic and ethological questions, the claimed purpose of which was to discover more about the springs of human action through the study of animals under experimental conditions.

Meanwhile, millions visited the zoos each year out of a curiosity which was both so large, so vague and so personal that it is hard to express in a single question. Today in France 22 million people visit the 200 zoos each year. A high proportion of the visitors were and are children.

Children in the industrialised world are surrounded by animal imagery: toys, cartoons, pictures, decorations of every sort. No other source of imagery can begin to compete with that of animals. The apparently spontaneous interest that children have in animals might lead one to suppose that this has always been the case. Certainly some of the earliest toys (when toys were unknown to the vast majority of the population) were animal. Equally, children's games, all over the world, include real or pretended animals. Yet it was not until the 19th century that reproductions of animals became a regular part of the decor of middle class childhoods — and then, in this century, with the advent of vast display and selling systems like Disney's — of all childhoods.

In the preceding centuries, the proportion of toys which were animal, was small. And these did not pretend to realism, but were symbolic. The difference was that between a traditional hobby horse and a rocking horse: the first was merely a stick with a rudimentary head which children rode like a broom handle: the second was an elaborate "reproduction" of a horse, painted realistically, with real reins of leather, a real mane of hair, and designed movement to resemble that of a horse galloping. The rocking horse was a 19th century invention.

20

This new demand for verisimilitude in animal toys led to different methods of manufacture. The first stuffed animals were produced, and the most expensive were covered with real animal skin — usually the skin of still-born calves. The same period saw the appearance of soft animals — bears, tigers, rabbits — such as children take to bed with them. Thus the manufacture of realistic animal toys coincides, more or less, with the establishment of public zoos.

The family visit to the zoo is often a more sentimental occasion than a visit to a fair or a football match. Adults take children to the zoo to show them the originals of their "reproductions", and also perhaps in the hope of re-finding some of the innocence of that reproduced animal world which they remember from their own childhood.

The animals seldom live up to the adults' memories, whilst to the children they appear, for the most part, unexpectedly lethargic and dull. (As frequent as the calls of animals in a zoo, are the cries of children demanding: Where is he? Why doesn't he move? Is he dead?) And so one might summarise the felt, but not necessarily expressed question of most visitors as: Why are these animals less than I believed?

And this unprofessional, unexpressed question is the one worth answering.

A zoo is a place where as many species and varieties of animal as possible are collected in order that they can be seen, observed, studied. In principle, each cage is a frame round the animal inside it. Visitors visit the zoo to look at animals. They proceed from cage to cage, not unlike visitors in an art gallery who stop in front of one painting, and then move on to the next or the one after next. Yet in the zoo the view is always wrong. Like an image out of focus. One is so accustomed to this that one scarcely notices it any more; or, rather, the apology habitually anticipates the disappointment, so that the latter is not felt. And the apology runs like this: What do you expect? It's not a dead object you have come to look at, it's alive. It's leading its own life. Why should this coincide with its being properly visible? Yet the reasoning of this apology is inadequate. The truth is more startling.

However you look at these animals, even if the animal is up against the bars, less than a foot from you, looking outwards in the public direction, *you are looking at something that has been rendered absolutely marginal*; and all the concentration you can muster will never be enough to centralise it. Why is this?

Within limits, the animals are free, but both they themselves, and their spectators, presume on their close confinement. The visibility through the glass, the spaces between the bars, or the empty air above the moat, are not what they seem — if they were, then everything would be changed. Thus visibility, space, air, have been reduced to tokens.

The decor, accepting these elements as tokens, sometimes reproduces them to create pure illusion — as in the case of painted prairies or painted rock pools at the back of the boxes for small animals. Sometimes it merely adds further tokens to suggest something of the animal's original landscape — the dead branches of a tree for monkeys, artificial rocks for bears, pebbles and shallow water for crocodiles. These added tokens serve two distinct purposes: for the spectator they are like theatre props: for the animal they constitute the bare minimum of an environment in which they can physically exist.

The animals, isolated from each other and without interaction between species, have become utterly dependent upon their keepers. Consequently most of their responses have been changed. What was central to their interest has been replaced by a passive waiting for a series of arbitrary outside interventions. The events they perceive occurring around them have become as illusory in terms of their natural responses, as the painted prairies. At the same time this very isolation (usually) guarantees their longevity as specimens and facilitates their taxonomic arrangement.

All this is what makes them marginal. The space which they inhabit is artificial. Hence their tendency to bundle towards the edge of it. (Beyond its edges there may be real space.) In some cages the light is equally artificial. In all cases the environment is illusory. Nothing surrounds them except their own lethargy or hyperactivity. They have nothing to act upon — except, briefly, supplied food and — very occasionally — a supplied mate. (Hence their perennial actions become marginal actions without an object.) Lastly, their dependence and isolation have so conditioned their responses that they treat any event which takes place around them — usually it is in front of them, where the public is — as marginal. (Hence their assumption of an otherwise exclusively human attitude — indifference.)

Zoos, realistic animal toys and the widespread commercial diffusion of animal imagery, all began as animals started to be withdrawn from daily life. One could suppose that such innovations were compensatory. Yet in reality the innovations themselves belonged to the same remorseless movement as was dispersing the animals. The zoos, with their theatrical decor for display, were in fact demonstrations of how animals had been rendered absolutely marginal. The realistic toys increased the demand for the new animal puppet: the urban pet. The reproduction of animals in images — as their biological reproduction in birth becomes a rarer and rarer sight — was competitively forced to make animals ever more exotic and remote.

Everywhere animals disappear. In zoos they constitute the living monument to their own disappearance. And in doing so, they provoked their last metaphor. *The Naked Ape, The Human Zoo,* are titles of world bestsellers. In these books the zoologist, Desmond Morris, proposes that the unnatural behaviour of animals in captivity can help us to understand, accept and overcome the stresses involved in living in consumer societies.

All sites of enforced marginalisation — ghettos, shanty towns, prisons, madhouses, concentration camps — have something in common with zoos. But it is both too easy and too evasive to use the zoo as a symbol. The zoo is a demonstration of the relations between man and animals; nothing else. The marginalisation of animals is today being followed by the marginalisation and disposal of the only class

24

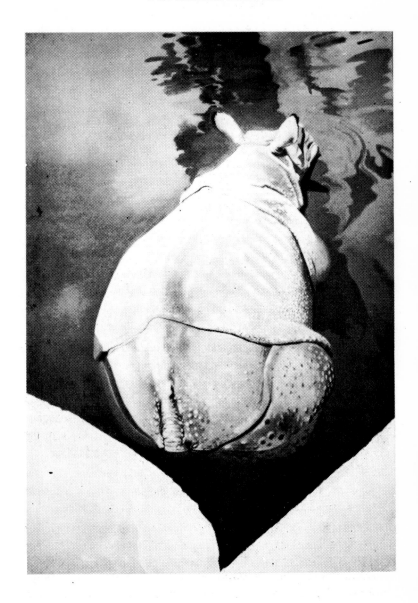

who, throughout history, has remained familiar with animals and maintained the wisdom which accompanies that familiarity: the middle and small peasant. The basis of this wisdom is an acceptance of the dualism at the very origin of the relation between man and animal. The rejection of this dualism is probably an important factor in opening the way to modern totalitarianism. But I do not wish to go beyond the limits of that unprofessional, unexpressed but fundamental question asked of the zoo.

The zoo cannot but disappoint. The public purpose of zoos is to offer visitors the opportunity of looking at animals. Yet nowhere in a zoo can a stranger encounter the look of an animal. At the most, the animal's gaze flickers and passes on. They look sideways. They look blindly beyond. They scan mechanically. They have been immunised to encounter, because nothing can any more occupy a *central* place in their attention.

Therein lies the ultimate consequence of their marginalisation. That look between animal and man, which may have played a crucial role in the development of human society, and with which, in any case, all men had always lived until less than a century ago, has been extinguished. Looking at each animal, the unaccompanied zoo visitor is alone. As for the crowds, they belong to a species which has at last been isolated.

This historic loss, to which zoos are a monument, is now irredeemable for the culture of capitalism.

1977

USES OF PHOTOGRAPHY

The Suit and the Photograph

What did August Sander tell his sitters before he took their pictures? And how did he say it so that they all believed him in the same way?

They each look at the camera with the same expression in their eyes. Insofar as there are differences, these are the results of the sitter's experience and character — the priest has lived a different life from the paper-hanger; but to all of them Sander's camera represents the same thing.

Did he simply say that their photographs were going to be a recorded part of history? And did he refer to history in such a way that their vanity and shyness dropped away, so that they looked into the lens telling themselves, using a strange historical tense: *I looked like this*. We cannot know. We simply have to recognise the uniqueness of his work, which he planned with the overall title of "Man of the 20th Century."

His full aim was to find, around Cologne in the area in which he was born in 1876, archetypes to represent every possible type, social class, sub-class, job, vocation, privilege. He hoped to take, in all, 600 portraits. His project was cut short by Hitler's Third Reich.

His son Erich, a socialist and anti-nazi was sent to a concentration camp where he died. The father hid his archives in the countryside. What remains today is an extraordinary social and human document. No other photographer, taking portraits of his own countrymen, has ever been so translucently documentary.

Walter Benjamin wrote in 1931 about Sander's work:

"It was not as a scholar, advised by race theorists or social researchers, that the author [Sander] undertook his enormous task, but, in the publisher's words, 'as the result of immediate observation.' It is indeed unprejudiced observation, bold and at the same time delicate, very much

in the spirit of Goethe's remark: 'There is a delicate form of the empirical which identifies itself so intimately with its object that it thereby becomes theory.' Accordingly it is quite proper that an observer like Döblin should light upon

precisely the scientific aspects of this opus and point out: 'Just as there is a comparative anatomy which enables one to understand the nature and history of organs, so here the photographer has produced a comparative photography, thereby gaining a scientific standpoint which places him beyond the photographer of detail.' It would be lamentable if economic circumstances prevented the further publication of this extraordinary corpus . . . Sander's work is more than a picture book, it is an atlas of instruction.''

In the inquiring spirit of Benjamin's remarks I want to examine Sander's well-known photograph of three young peasants on the road in the evening, going to a dance. There is as much descriptive information in this image as in pages by a descriptive master like Zola. Yet I only want to consider one thing: their suits.

The date is 1914. The three young men belong, at the very most, to the second generation who ever wore such suits in the European countryside. Twenty or 30 years earlier, such clothes did not exist at a price which peasants could afford. Among the young today, formal dark suits have become rare in the villages of at least western Europe. But for most of this century most peasants — and most workers — wore dark three-piece suits on ceremonial occasions, Sundays and fêtes.

When I go to a funeral in the village where I live, the men of my age and older are still wearing them. Of course there have been modifications of fashion: the width of trousers and lapels, the length of jackets change. Yet the physical character of the suit and its message does not change.

Let us first consider its physical character. Or, more precisely, its physical character when worn by village peasants. And to make generalisation more convincing, let us look at a second photograph of a village band.

Sander took this group portrait in 1913, yet it could well have been the band at the dance for which the three with their walking sticks are setting out along the road. Now make an experiment. Block out the faces of the band with a piece of paper, and consider only their clothed bodies.

By no stretch of the imagination can you believe that these bodies belong to the middle or ruling class. They might belong to workers, rather than peasants; but otherwise there is no doubt. Nor is the clue their hands — as it would be if you could touch them. Then why is their class so apparent?

Is it a question of fashion and the quality of the cloth of their suits? In real life such details would be telling. In a small black and white photograph they are not very evident. Yet the static photograph shows, perhaps more vividly than in life, the fundamental reason why the suits, far from

30

disguising the social class of those who wore them, underlined and emphasised it.

Their suits deform them. Wearing them, they look as though they were physically mis-shapen. A past style in clothes often looks absurd until it is re-incorporated into fashion. Indeed the economic logic of fashion depends on making the old-fashioned look absurd. But here we are not faced primarily with that kind of absurdity; here the clothes look less absurd, less "abnormal" than the men's bodies which are in them.

The musicians give the impression of being uncoordinated, bandy-legged, barrel-chested, low-arsed, twisted or scalene. The violinist on the right is made to look almost like a dwarf. None of their abnormalities is extreme. They do not provoke pity. They are just sufficient to undermine physical dignity. We look at bodies which appear coarse, clumsy, brute-like. And incorrigibly so.

Now make the experiment the other way round. Cover the bodies of the band and look only at their faces. They are country faces. Nobody could suppose that they are a group of barristers or managing directors. They are five men from a village who like to make music and do so with a certain self-respect. As we look at the faces we can imagine what the bodies would look like. And what we imagine is quite different from what we have just seen. In imagination we see them as their parents might remember them when absent. We accord them the normal dignity they have.

To make the point clearer, let us now consider an image where tailored clothes, instead of deforming, *preserve* the physical identity and therefore the natural authority of those wearing them. I have deliberately chosen a Sander photograph which looks old-fashioned and could easily lend itself to parody: the photograph of four Protestant missionaries in 1931.

Despite the portentousness, it is not even necessary to

make the experiment of blocking out the faces. It is clear that here the suits actually confirm and enhance the physical presence of those wearing them. The clothes convey the same message as the faces and as the history of the bodies they hide. Suits, experience, social formation and function coincide.

Look back now at the three on the road to the dance. Their hands look too big, their bodies too thin, their legs too short. (They use their walking sticks as though they were driving cattle.) We can make the same experiment with the faces and the effect is exactly the same as with the band. They can wear only their hats as if they suited them.

Where does this lead us? Simply to the conclusion that peasants can't buy good suits and don't know how to wear them? No, what is at issue here is a graphic, if small, example (perhaps one of the most graphic which exists) of what Gramsci called class hegemony. Let us look at the contradictions involved more closely.

Most peasants, if not suffering from malnutrition, are physically strong and well-developed. Well-developed because of the very varied hard physical work they do. It would be too simple to make a list of physical characteristics — broad hands through working with them from a very early age, broad shoulders relative to the body through the habit of carrying, and so on. In fact many variations and exceptions also exist. One can, however, speak of a characteristic physical rhythm which most peasants, both women and men, acquire.

This rhythm is directly related to the energy demanded by the amount of work which has to be done in a day, and is reflected in typical physical movements and stance. It is an extended sweeping rhythm. Not necessarily slow. The traditional acts of scything or sawing may exemplify it. The

33

way peasants ride horses makes it distinctive, as also the way they walk, as if testing the earth with each stride. In addition peasants possess a special physical dignity: this is determined by a kind of functionalism, a way of being *fully at home in effort.*

The suit, as we know it today, developed in Europe as a professional ruling class costume in the last third of the 19th century. Almost anonymous as a uniform, it was the first ruling class costume to idealise purely *sedentary* power. The power of the administrator and conference table. Essentially the suit was made for the gestures of talking and calculating abstractly. (As distinct, compared to previous upper class costumes, from the gestures of riding, hunting, dancing, duelling.)

It was the English *gentleman,* with all the apparent restraint which that new stereotype implied, who launched the suit. It was a costume which inhibited vigorous action, and which action ruffled, uncreased and spoilt. "Horses sweat, men perspire and women glow." By the turn of the century, and increasingly after the first world war, the suit was mass-produced for mass urban and rural markets.

The physical contradiction is obvious. Bodies which are fully at home in effort, bodies which are used to extended sweeping movement: clothes idealising the sedentary, the discrete, the effortless. I would be the last to argue for a return to traditional peasant costumes. Any such return is bound to be escapist, for these costumes were a form of capital handed down through generations, and in the world today, in which every corner is dominated by the market, such a principle is anachronistic.

We can note, however, how traditional peasant working or ceremonial clothes respected the specific character of the bodies they were clothing. They were in general loose, and only tight in places where they were gathered to allow for freer movement. They were the antithesis of tailored clothes, clothes cut to follow the idealised shape of a more or less stationary body and then to hang from it!

Yet nobody forced peasants to buy suits, and the three on their way to the dance are clearly proud of them. They wear them with a kind of panache. This is exactly why the suit might become a classic and easily taught example of class hegemony.

Villagers — and, in a different way, city workers — were persuaded to choose suits. By publicity. By pictures. By the new mass media. By salesmen. By example. By the sight of new kinds of travellers. And also by political developments of accommodation and state central organisation. For example: in 1900, on the occasion of the great Universal Exhibition, all the mayors of France were, for the first time ever, invited to a banquet in Paris. Most of them were the peasant mayors of village communes. Nearly 30,000 came! And, naturally, for the occasion the vast majority wore suits.

The working classes — but peasants were simpler and more naïve about it than workers — came to accept *as their own* certain standards of the class that ruled over them — in this case standards of chic and sartorial worthiness. At the same time their very acceptance of these standards, their very conforming to these norms which had nothing to do with either their own inheritance or their daily experience, condemned them, within the system of those standards, to being always, and recognisably to the classes above them, second-rate, clumsy, uncouth, defensive. That indeed is to succumb to a cultural hegemony.

Perhaps one can nevertheless propose that when the three arrived and had drunk a beer or two, and had eyed the girls (whose clothes had not yet changed so drastically), they

35

hung up their jackets, took off their ties, and danced, maybe wearing their hats, until the morning and the next day's work.

1979

Photographs of Agony

The news from Vietnam did not make big headlines in the papers this morning. It was simply reported that the American air force is systematically pursuing its policy of bombing the north. Yesterday there were 270 raids.

Behind this report there is an accumulation of other information. The day before yesterday the American air force launched the heaviest raids of this month. So far more bombs have been dropped this month than during any other comparable period. Among the bombs being dropped are the seven-ton superbombs, each of which flattens an area of approximately 8,000 square metres. Along with the large bombs, various kinds of small antipersonnel bombs are being dropped. One kind is full of plastic barbs which, having ripped through the flesh and embedded themselves in the body, cannot be located by x-ray. Another is called the Spider: a small bomb like a grenade with almost invisible 30-centimetre-long antennae, which, if touched, act as detonators. These bombs, distributed over the ground where larger explosions have taken place, are designed to blow up survivors who run to put out the fires already burning, or go to help those already wounded.

There are no pictures from Vietnam in the papers today. But there is a photograph taken by Donald McCullin in Hue in 1968 which could have been printed with the reports this morning. (See *The Destruction Business* by Donald McCullin, London, 1972.) It shows an old man squatting with a child in his arms, both of them are bleeding profusely with the black blood of black-and-white photographs.

In the last year or so, it has become normal for certain mass circulation newspapers to publish war photographs which earlier would have been suppressed as being too shocking. One might explain this development by arguing

37

that these newspapers have come to realise that a large section of their readers are now aware of the horrors of war and want to be shown the truth. Alternatively, one might argue that these newspapers believe that their readers have become inured to violent images and so now compete in terms of ever more violent sensationalism.

The first argument is too idealistic and the second too transparently cynical. Newspapers now carry violent war photographs because their effect, except in rare cases, is not what it was once presumed to be. A paper like the *Sunday Times* continues to publish shocking photographs about Vietnam or about Northern Ireland whilst politically supporting the policies responsible for the violence. This is why we have to ask: What effect do such photographs have?

Many people would argue that such photographs remind us shockingly of the reality, the lived reality, behind the abstractions of political theory, casualty statistics or news bulletins. Such photographs, they might go on to say, are printed on the black curtain which is drawn across what we choose to forget or refuse to know. According to them, McCullin serves as an eye we cannot shut. Yet what is it that they make us see?

They bring us up short. The most literal adjective that could be applied to them is *arresting*. We are seized by them. (I am aware that there are people who pass them over, but about them there is nothing to say.) As we look at them, the moment of the other's suffering engulfs us. We are filled with either despair or indignation. Despair takes on some of the other's suffering to no purpose. Indignation demands action. We try to emerge from the moment of the photograph back into our lives. As we do so, the contrast is such that the resumption of our lives appears to be a hopelessly inadequate response to what we have just seen.

McCullin's most typical photographs record sudden moments of agony — a terror, a wounding, a death, a cry of grief. These moments are in reality utterly discontinuous with normal time. It is the knowledge that such moments are probable and the anticipation of them that makes "time" in the front line unlike all other experiences of time. The camera which isolates a moment of agony isolates no more violently than the experience of that moment isolates itself. The word *trigger,* applied to rifle and camera, reflects a correspondence which does not stop at the purely mechanical. The image seized by the camera is doubly violent and both violences reinforce the same contrast: the contrast between the photographed moment and all others.

As we emerge from the photographed moment back into our lives, we do not realise this; we assume that the discontinuity is our responsibility. The truth is that any response to that photographed moment is bound to be felt as inadequate. Those who are there in the situation being photographed, those who hold the hand of the dying or staunch a wound, are not seeing the moment as we have and their responses are of an altogether different order. It is not possible for anyone to look pensively at such a moment and to emerge stronger. McCullin, whose "contemplation" is both dangerous and active, writes bitterly underneath a photograph: "I only use the camera like I use a toothbrush. It does the job."

The possible contradictions of the war photograph now become apparent. It is generally assumed that its purpose is to awaken concern. The most extreme examples — as in most of McCullin's work — show moments of agony in order to extort the maximum concern. Such moments, whether photographed or not, are discontinuous with all other moments. They exist by themselves. But the reader

39

who has been arrested by the photograph may tend to feel this discontinuity as his own personal moral inadequacy. *And as soon as this happens even his sense of shock is dispersed*: his own moral inadequacy may now shock him as much as the crimes being committed in the war. Either he shrugs off this sense of inadequacy as being only too familiar, or else he thinks of performing a kind of penance — of which the purest example would be to make a contribution to OXFAM or to UNICEF.

In both cases, the issue of the war which has caused that moment is effectively depoliticised. The picture becomes evidence of the general human condition. It accuses nobody and everybody.

Confrontation with a photographed moment of agony can mask a far more extensive and urgent confrontation. Usually the wars which we are shown are being fought directly or indirectly in "our" name. What we are shown horrifies us. The next step should be for us to confront our own lack of political freedom. In the political systems as they exist, we have no legal opportunity of effectively influencing the conduct of wars waged in our name. To realise this and to act accordingly is the only effective way of responding to what the photograph shows. Yet the double violence of the photographed moment actually works against this realisation. That is why they can be published with impunity.

1972

Paul Strand

There is a widespread assumption that if one is interested in the visual, one's interest must be limited to a technique of somehow *treating* the visual. Thus the visual is divided into categories of special interest: painting, photography, real appearances, dreams and so on. And what is forgotten — like all essential questions in a positivist culture — is the meaning and enigma of visibility itself.

I think of this now because I want to describe what I can see in two books which are in front of me. They are two volumes of a retrospective monograph on the work of Paul Strand. The first photographs date from 1915, when Strand was a sort of pupil of Alfred Stieglitz; the most recent ones were taken in 1968.

The earliest works deal mostly with people and sites in New York. The first of them shows a half-blind beggar woman. One of her eyes is opaque, the other sharp and wary. Round her neck she wears a label with BLIND printed on it. It is an image with a clear social message. But it is something else, too. We shall see later that in all Strand's best photographs of people, he presents us with the visible evidence, not just of their presence, but of their *life*. At one level, such evidence of a life is social comment — Strand has consistently taken a left political position — but, at a different level, such evidence serves to suggest visually the totality of another lived life, from within which we ourselves are no more than a sight. This is why the black letters B-L-I-N-D on a white label do more than spell the word. While the picture remains in front of us, we can never take them as read. The earliest image in the book forces us to reflect on the significance of seeing itself.

The next section of photographs, from the 1920s, includes photographs of machine parts and close-ups of various natural forms — roots, rocks and grasses. Already Strand's technical perfectionism and strong aesthetic interests are apparent. But equally his obstinate, resolute respect for the thing-in-itself is also apparent. And the result is often disconcerting. Some would say that these photographs fail, for they remain details of what they have been taken from: they never become independent images. Nature, in these photographs, is intransigent to art, and the machine-details mock the stillness of their perfectly rendered images.

From the 1930s onwards, the photographs fall typically into groups associated with journeys that Strand made: to Mexico, New England, France, Italy, the Hebrides, Egypt, Ghana, Rumania. These are the photographs for which Strand has become well-known, and it is on the evidence of these photographs that he should be considered a great photographer. With these black-and-white photographs, with these records which are distributable anywhere, he offers us the sight of a number of places and people in such a way that our view of the world can be qualitatively extended.

The social approach of Strand's photography to reality might be called documentary or neo-realist in so far as its obvious cinematic equivalent is to be found in the prewar films of Flaherty or the immediate postwar Italian films of de Sica or Rossellini. This means that on his travels Strand avoids the picturesque, the panoramic, and tries to find a city in a street, the way of life of a nation in the corner of a kitchen. In one or two pictures of power dams and some "heroic" portraits he gives way to the romanticism of Soviet socialist realism. But mostly his approach lets him choose ordinary subjects which in their ordinariness are extraordinarily representative.

He has an infallible eye for the quintessential: whether it

is to be found on a Mexican doorstep, or in the way that an Italian village schoolgirl in a black pinafore holds her straw hat. Such photographs enter so deeply into the particular that they reveal to us the stream of a culture or a history which is flowing through that particular subject like blood. The images of these photographs, once seen, subsist in our mind until some actual incident, which we witness or live, refers to one of them as though to a more solid reality. But it is not this which makes Strand as a photographer unique.

His method as a photographer is more unusual. One could say that it was the antithesis to Henri Cartier-Bresson's. The photographic moment for Cartier-Bresson is an instant, a fraction of a second, and he stalks that instant as though it were a wild animal. The photographic moment for Strand is a biographical or historic moment, whose duration is ideally measured not by seconds but by its relation to a lifetime. Strand does not pursue an instant, but encourages a moment to arise as one might encourage a story to be told.

In practical terms this means that he decides what he wants before he takes the picture, never plays with the accidental, works slowly, hardly ever crops a picture, often still uses a plate camera, formally asks people to pose for him. His pictures are all remarkable for their intentionality. His portraits are very frontal. The subject is looking at us; we are looking at the subject; it has been arranged like that. But there is a similar sense of frontality in many of his other pictures of landscapes or objects or buildings. His camera is not free-roving. He chooses where to place it.

Where he has chosen to place it is not where something is about to happen, but where a number of happenings will be related. Thus, without any use of anecdote, he turns his subjects into narrators. The river narrates itself. The field

43

where the horses are grazing recounts itself. The wife tells the story of her marriage. In each case Strand, the photographer, has chosen the place to put his camera as listener.

The approach: neo-realist. The method: deliberate, frontal, formal, with every surface thoroughly scanned. What is the result?

His best photographs are unusually dense — not in the sense of being over-burdened or obscure, but in the sense of being filled with an unusual amount of substance per square inch. And all this substance becomes the stuff of the life of the subject. Take the famous portrait of Mr Bennett from Vermont, New England. His jacket, his shirt, the stubble on his chin, the timber of the house behind, the air around him become in this image the face of his life, of which his actual facial expression is the concentrated spirit. It is the whole photograph, frowning, which surveys us.

44

A Mexican woman sits against a wall. She has a woollen shawl over her head and shoulders and a broken plaited basket on her lap. Her skirt is patched and the wall behind her very shabby. The only fresh surface in the picture is that of her face. Once again, the surfaces we read with our eyes

become the actual chafing texture of her daily life; once again the photograph is a panel of her being. At first sight the image is soberly materialist, but just as her body wears through her clothes and the load in the basket wears away the basket, and passers-by have rubbed off the surface of the wall, so her being as a woman (her own existence for herself) begins, as one goes on looking at the picture, to rub through the materialism of the image.

A young Rumanian peasant and his wife lean against a wooden fence. Above and behind them, diffused in the light, is a field and, above that, a small modern house, totally insignificant as architecture, and the grey silhouette of a nondescript tree beside it. Here it is not the substantiality of surfaces which fills every square inch but a Slav sense of distance, a sense of plains or hills that continue indefinitely. And, once more, it is impossible to separate this quality from the presence of the two figures; it is there in the angle of his hat, the long extended movement of his arms, the flowers embroidered on her waistcoat, the way her hair is tied up; it is there across the width of their wide faces and mouths. What informs the whole photograph — space — is part of the skin of their lives.

These photographs depend upon Strand's technical skill, his ability to select, his knowledge of the places he visits, his eye, his sense of timing, his use of the camera; but he might have all these talents and still not be capable of producing such pictures. What has finally determined his success in his photographs of people and in his landscapes — which are only extensions of people who happen to be invisible — is his ability to invite the narrative: to present himself to his subject in such a way that the subject is willing to say: *I am as you see me.*

This is more complicated than it may seem. The present

tense of the verb *to be* refers only to the present; but nevertheless, with the first person singular in front of it, it absorbs the past which is inseparable from the pronoun. *I am* includes all that has made me so. It is more than a statement of immediate fact: it is already an explanation, a justification, a demand — it is already autobiographical. Strand's photographs suggest his sitters trust him to *see* their life story. And it is for this reason that, although the portraits are formal and posed, there is no need, either on the part of photographer or photograph, for the disguise of a borrowed role.

Photography, because it preserves the appearance of an event or a person, has always been closely associated with the idea of the historical. The ideal of photography, aesthetics apart, is to seize an "historic" moment. But Paul Strand's relation as a photographer to the historic is a unique one. His photographs convey a unique sense of duration. The *I am* is given its time in which to reflect on the past and to anticipate its future: the exposure time does no violence to the time of the *I am*: on the contrary, one has the strange impression that the exposure time *is* the lifetime.

1972

Uses of Photography

For Susan Sontag

I want to write down some of my responses to Susan Sontag's book *On Photography*. All the quotations I will use are from her text. The thoughts are sometimes my own, but all originate in the experience of reading her book.

The camera was invented by Fox Talbot in 1839. Within a mere 30 years of its invention as a gadget for an elite, photography was being used for police filing, war reporting, military reconnaissance, pornography, encyclopedic documentation, family albums, postcards, anthropological records (often, as with the Indians in the United States, accompanied by genocide), sentimental moralising, inquisitive probing (the wrongly named "candid camera"): aesthetic effects, news reporting and formal portraiture. The first cheap popular camera was put on the market, a little later, in 1888. The speed with which the possible uses of photography were seized upon is surely an indication of photography's profound, central applicability to industrial capitalism. Marx came of age the year of the camera's invention.

It was not, however, until the 20th century and the period between the two world wars that the photograph became the dominant and most "natural" way of referring to appearances. It was then that it replaced the world as immediate testimony. It was the period when photography was thought of as being most transparent, offering direct access to the real: the period of the great witnessing masters of the medium like Paul Strand and Walker Evans. It was, in the capitalist countries, the freest moment of photography: it had been liberated from the limitations of fine art, and it had become a public medium which could be used democratically.

Yet the moment was brief. The very "truthfulness" of the

48

new medium encouraged its deliberate use as a means of propaganda. The Nazis were among the first to use systematic photographic propaganda.

"Photographs are perhaps the most mysterious of all the objects that make up and thicken the environment we recognise as modern. Photographs really are experience captured, and the camera is the ideal arm of consciousness in its acquisitive mood."

In the first period of its existence photography offered a new technical opportunity; it was an implement. Now, instead of offering new choices, its usage and its "reading" were becoming habitual, an unexamined part of modern perception itself. Many developments contributed to this transformation. The new film industry. The invention of the lightweight camera — so that the taking of a photograph ceased to be a ritual and became a "reflex". The discovery of photojournalism — whereby the text follows the pictures instead of vice versa. The emergence of advertising as a crucial economic force.

"Through photographs, the world becomes a series of unrelated, free-standing particles; and history, past and present, a set of anecdotes and *faits divers*. The camera makes reality atomic, manageable, and opaque. It is a view of the world which denies interconnectedness, continuity, but which confers on each moment the character of a mystery."

The first mass-media magazine was started in the United States in 1936. At least two things were prophetic about the launching of *Life*, the prophecies to be fully realised in the postwar television age. The new picture magazine was financed not by its sales, but by the advertising it carried. A third of its images were devoted to publicity. The second prophecy lay in its title. This is ambiguous. It may mean that the pictures inside are about life. Yet it seems to promise more: that these pictures *are* life. The first photograph in the first number played on this ambiguity. It showed a newborn baby. The caption underneath read: "Life begins . . ."

What served in place of the photograph; before the camera's invention? The expected answer is the engraving, the drawing, the painting. The more revealing answer might be: memory. What photographs do out there in space was previously done within reflection.

"Proust somewhat misconstrues that photographs are, not so much an instrument of memory as an invention of it or a replacement."

Unlike any other visual image, a photograph is not a rendering, an imitation or an interpretation of its subject, but actually a trace of it. No painting or drawing, however naturalist, *belongs* to its subject in the way that a photograph does.

"A photograph is not only an image (as a painting is an image), an interpretation of the real; it is also a trace, something directly stencilled off the real, like a footprint or a death mask."

Human visual perception is a far more complex and selective process than that by which a film records. Nevertheless the camera lens and the eye both register images — because of their sensitivity to light — at great speed and in the face of an immediate event. What the camera does, however, and what the eye in itself can never do, is to *fix* the appearance of that event. It removes its appearance from the flow of appearances and it preserves it, not perhaps for ever but for as long as the film exists. The essential character of this preservation is not dependent upon the image being static; unedited film rushes preserve in essentially the same way The camera saves a set of appearances from the otherwise inevitable supercession of further appearances. It holds them unchanging. And before the invention of the camera nothing could do this, except, in the mind's eye, the faculty of memory.

I am not saying that memory is a kind of film. That is a banal simile. From the comparison film/memory we learn nothing about the latter. What we learn is how strange and unprecedented was the procedure of photography.

Yet, unlike memory, photographs do not in themselves preserve meaning. They offer appearances — with all the credibility and gravity we normally lend to appearances — prised away from their meaning. Meaning is the result of understanding functions. "And functioning takes place in time, and must be explained in time. Only that which narrates can make us understand." Photographs in themselves do not narrate. Photographs preserve instant appearances. Habit now protects us against the shock involved in such preservation. Compare the exposure time for a film with the life of the print made, and let us assume that the print only lasts ten years: the ratio for an average modern photograph would be approximately 20,000,000,000: 1. Perhaps that can serve as a reminder of the violence of the fission whereby appearances are separated by the camera from their function.

We must now distinguish between two quite distinct uses of photography. There are photographs which belong to private experience and there are those which are used publicly. The private photograph — the portrait of a mother, a picture of a daughter, a group photo of one's own team — is appreciated and read in a context *which is continuous with that from which the camera removed it.* (The violence of the removal is sometimes felt as incredulousness:

51

"Was that really Dad?'') Nevertheless such a photograph remains surrounded by the meaning from which it was severed. A mechanical device, the camera has been used as an instrument to contribute to a living memory. The photograph is a memento from a life being lived.

The contemporary public photograph usually presents an event, a seized set of appearances, which has nothing to do with us, its readers, or with the original meaning of the event. It offers information, but information severed from all lived experience. If the public photograph contributes to a memory, it is to the memory of an unknowable and total stranger. The violence is expressed in that strangeness. It records an instant sight about which this stranger has shouted: Look!

Who is the stranger? One might answer: the photographer. Yet if one considers the entire use-system of photographed images, the answer of "the photographer" is clearly inadequate. Nor can one reply: those who use the

52

photographs. It is because the photographs carry no certain meaning in themselves, because they are like images in the memory of a total stranger, that they lend themselves to any use.

Daumier's famous cartoon of Nadar in his balloon suggests an answer. Nadar is travelling through the sky above Paris — the wind has blown off his hat — and he is photographing with his camera the city and its people below.

Has the camera replaced the eye of God? The decline of religion corresponds with the rise of the photograph. Has the culture of capitalism telescoped God into photography? The transformation would not be as surprising as it may at first seem.

The faculty of memory led men everywhere to ask

whether, just as they themselves could preserve certain events from oblivion, there might not be other eyes noting and recording otherwise unwitnessed events. Such eyes they then accredited to their ancestors, to spirits, to gods or to their single deity. What was seen by this supernatural eye was inseparably linked with the principle of justice. It was possible to escape the justice of men, but not this higher justice from which nothing or little could be hidden.

Memory implies a certain act of redemption. What is remembered has been saved from nothingness. What is forgotten has been abandoned. If all events are seen, instantaneously, outside time, by a supernatural eye, the distinction between remembering and forgetting is transformed into an act of judgment, into the rendering of justice, whereby recognition is close to *being remembered,* and condemnation is close to *being forgotten.* Such a presentiment, extracted from man's long, painful experience of time, is to be found in varying forms in almost every culture and religion, and, very clearly, in Christianity.

At first, the secularisation of the capitalist world during the 19th century elided the judgment of God into the judgment of History in the name of Progress. Democracy and Science became the agents of such a judgment. And for a brief moment, photography, as we have seen, was considered to be an aid to these agents. It is still to this historical moment that photography owes its ethical reputation as Truth.

During the second half of the 20th century the judgment of history has been abandoned by all except the under-privileged and dispossessed. The industrialised, "developed" world, terrified of the past, blind to the future, lives within an opportunism which has emptied the principle of justice of all credibility. Such opportunism turns

54

everything — nature, history, suffering, other people, catastrophes, sport, sex, politics — into spectacle. And the implement used to do this — until the act becomes so habitual that the conditioned imagination may do it alone — is the camera.

"Our very sense of situation is now articulated by the camera's interventions. The omnipresence of cameras persuasively suggests that time consists of interesting events, events worth photographing. This, in turn, makes it easy to feel that any event, once underway, and whatever its moral character, should be allowed to complete itself — so that something else can be brought into the world, the photograph."

The spectacle creates an eternal present of immediate expectation: memory ceases to be necessary or desirable. With the loss of memory the continuities of meaning and judgment are also lost to us. The camera relieves us of the burden of memory. It surveys us like God, and it surveys for us. Yet no other god has been so cynical, for the camera records in order to forget.

Susan Sontag locates this god very clearly in history. He is the god of monopoly capitalism.

"A capitalist society requires a culture based on images. It needs to furnish vast amounts of entertainment in order to stimulate buying and anaesthetise the injuries of class, race and sex. And it needs to gather unlimited amounts of information, the better to exploit the natural resources, increase productivity, keep order, make war, give jobs to bureaucrats. The camera's twin capacities, to subjectivise reality and to objectify it, ideally serve these needs and strengthen them. Cameras define reality in the two ways essential to the workings of an advanced industrial society:

as a spectacle (for masses) and as an object of surveillance (for rulers). The production of images also furnishes a ruling ideology. Social change is replaced by a change in images.''

Her theory of the current use of photographs leads one to ask whether photography might serve a different function. Is there an alternative photographic practice? The question should not be answered naively. Today no alternative professional practice (if one thinks of the profession of photographer) is possible. The system can accommodate any photograph. Yet it may be possible to begin to use photographs according to a practice addressed to an alternative future. This future is a hope which we need now, if we are to maintain a struggle, a resistance, against the societies and culture of capitalism.

Photographs have often been used as a radical weapon in posters, newspapers, pamphlets, and so on. I do not wish to belittle the value of such agitational publishing. Yet the current systematic public use of photography needs to be challenged, not simply by turning round like a cannon and aiming it at different targets, but by changing its practice. How?

We need to return to the distinction I made between the private and public uses of photography. In the private use of photography, the context of the instant recorded is preserved so that the photograph lives in an ongoing continuity. (If you have a photograph of Peter on your wall, you are not likely to forget what Peter means to you.) The public photograph, by contrast, is torn from its context, and becomes a dead object which, exactly because it is dead, lends itself to any arbitrary use.

In the most famous photographic exhibition ever organised, *The Family of Man* (put together by Edward Steichen in 1955), photographs from all over the world were presented as though they formed a universal family album. Steichen's intuition was absolutely correct: the private use of photographs . can be exemplary for their public use. Unfortunately the shortcut he took in treating the existing class-divided world as if it were a family, inevitably made the whole exhibition, not necessarily each picture, sentimental and complacent. The truth is that most photographs taken of people are about suffering, and most of that suffering is man-made.

"One's first encounter," writes Susan Sontag, "with the photographic inventory of ultimate horror is a kind of revelation, the prototypically modern revelation: a negative epiphany. For me, it was photographs of Bergen-Belsen and Dachau which I came across by chance in a bookstore in Santa Monica in July 1945. Nothing I have seen — in photographs or in real life — ever cut me as sharply, deeply, instantaneously. Indeed, it seems plausible to me to divide my life into two parts, before I saw those photographs (I was twelve) and after, though it was several years before I understood fully what they were about."

Photographs are relics of the past, traces of what has happened. If the living take that past upon themselves, if the past becomes an integral part of the process of people making their own history, then all photographs would re-acquire a living context, they would continue to exist in time, instead of being arrested moments. It is just possible that photography is the prophecy of a human memory yet to be socially and politically achieved. Such a memory would encompass any image of the past, however tragic, however guilty, within its own continuity. The distinction between the private and public uses of photography would be transcended. The Family of Man would exist.

Meanwhile we live today in the world as it is. Yet this possible prophecy of photography indicates the direction in which any alternative use of photography needs to develop. The task of an alternative photography is to incorporate photography into social and political memory, instead of using it as a substitute which encourages the atrophy of any such memory.

The task will determine both the kinds of pictures taken and the way they are used. There can of course be no formulae, no prescribed practice. Yet in recognising how photography has come to be used by capitalism, we can define at least some of the principles of an alternative practice.

For the photographer this means thinking of her or himself not so much as a reporter to the rest of the world but, rather, as a recorder for those involved in the events photographed. The distinction is crucial.

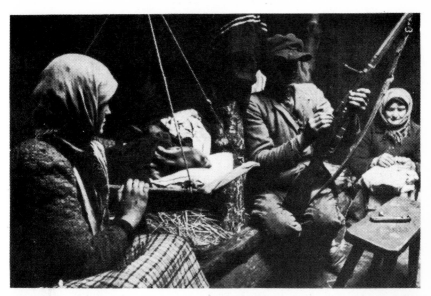

What makes these photographs so tragic and extra-ordinary is that, looking at them, one is convinced that they were not taken to please generals, to boost the morale of a civilian public, to glorify heroic soldiers or to shock the world press: they were images addressed to those suffering what they depict. And given this integrity towards and with their subject matter, such photographs later became a memorial, to the 20 million Russians killed in the war, for those who mourn them. (See *Russian War Photographs 1941 - 45*. Text by A. J. P. Taylor, London 1978.) The unifying horror of a total people's war made such .an attitude on the part of the war photographers (and even the censors) a natural one. Photographers, however, can work with a similar attitude in less extreme circumstances.

The alternative use of photographs which already exist leads us back once more to the phenomenon and faculty of memory. The aim must be to construct a context for a photograph, to construct it with words, to construct it with other photographs, to construct it by its place in an ongoing text of photographs and images. How? Normally photographs are used in a very unilinear way — they are used to illustrate an argument, or to demonstrate a thought which goes like this:

$$\longrightarrow$$

Very frequently also they are used tautologically so that the photograph merely repeats what is being said in words. Memory is not unilinear at all. Memory works radially, that is to say with an enormous number of associations all leading to the same event. The diagram is like this:

$$\ast$$

If we want to put a photograph back into the context of experience, social experience, social memory, we have to respect the laws of memory. We have to situate the printed photograph so that it acquires something of the surprising conclusiveness of that which *was* and *is*.

What Brecht wrote about acting in one of his poems is applicable to such a practice. For *instant* one can read photography, for *acting* the re-creating of context:

So you should simply make the instant
Stand out, without in the process hiding
What you are making it stand out from.
    Give your acting
That progression of one-thing-after-another,
    that attitude of
Working up what you have taken on. In this way
You will show the flow of events and also the course
Of your work, permitting the spectator
To experience this Now on many levels, coming from
    Previously and
Merging into Afterwards, also having much else Now
Alongside it. He is sitting not only
In your theatre but also
In the world.

There are a few great photographs which practically achieve this by themselves. But any photograph may become such a 'Now' if an adequate context is created for it. In general the better the photograph, the fuller the context which can be created.

Such a context replaces the photograph in time — not its own original time for that is impossible — but in narrated time. Narrated time becomes historic time when it is assumed by social memory and social action. The

61

constructed narrated time needs to respect the process of memory which it hopes to stimulate.

There is never a single approach to something remembered. The remembered is not like a terminus at the end of a line. Numerous approaches or stimuli converge

upon it and lead to it. Words, comparisons, signs need to create a context for a printed photograph in a comparable way; that is to say, they must mark and leave open diverse approaches. A radial system has to be constructed around the photograph so that it may be seen in terms which are simultaneously personal, political, economic, dramatic, everyday and historic.

1978

MOMENTS LIVED

The Primitive and the Professional

Art-historically the word *primitive* has been used in three different ways: to designate art (before Raphael) on the borderline between the medieval and modern Renaissance traditions; to label the trophies and "curiosities" taken from the colonies (Africa, Caribbean, South Pacific) when brought back to the imperial metropolis; and lastly to put in its place the art of men and women from the working classes — proletarian, peasant, petit-bourgeois — who did not leave their class by becoming *professional* artists. According to all three usages of the word, originating in the last century when the confidence of the European ruling class was at its height, the superiority of the main European tradition of secular art, serving that same "civilised" ruling class, was assured.

Most professional artists begin their training when young. Most primitive artists of the third category come to painting or sculpture in middle or even old age. Their art usually derives from considerable personal experience and, indeed, is often provoked as a result of the profundity or intensity of that experience. Yet artistically their art is seen as naïve, that is, inexperienced. It is the significance of this contradiction that we need to understand. Does it actually exist, and if so, what does it mean? To talk of the dedication of the primitive artist, his patience and his application amounting to a kind of skill, does not altogether answer the question.

The primitive is defined as the non-professional. The category of the professional artist, as distinct from the master craftsman, was not clear until the 17th century. (And in some places, especially in Eastern Europe, not until the 19th century.) The distinction between profession and craft is at first difficult to make, yet it is of great importance. The

64

craftsman survives so long as the standards for judging his work are shared by different classes. The professional appears when it is necessary for the craftsman to leave his class and "emigrate" to the ruling class, whose standards of judgement are different.

The relationship of the professional artist to the class that ruled or aspired to rule was complicated, various and should not be simplified. His training however — and it was his training which made him a professional — taught him a set of conventional skills. That is to say, he became skilled in using a set of conventions. Conventions of composition, drawing, perspective, chiaroscuro, anatomy, poses, symbolism. And these conventions corresponded so closely to the social experience — or anyway to the social manners — of the class he was serving, that they were not even seen as conventions but were thought of as the only way of recording and preserving eternal truths. Yet to the other social classes such professional painting appeared to be so remote from their own experience, that they saw it as a mere social convention, a mere accoutrement of the class that ruled over them: which is why in moments of revolt, painting and sculpture were often destroyed.

During the 19th century certain artists, for consciously social or political reasons, tried to extend the professional tradition of painting, so that it might express the experience of other classes (for example, Millet, Courbet, Van Gogh). Their personal struggles, their failures, and the opposition they met with, were a measure of the enormity of the undertaking. Perhaps one pedestrian example will give some idea of the extent of the difficulties involved. Consider Ford Madox Brown's well-known painting of *Work* in Manchester Art Gallery. It shows a team of navvies, with passers-by and bystanders, working on a sidewalk. It took the painter ten years to complete, and it is, at one level, extremely accurate. But it looks like a religious scene — the Mounting of the Cross, or the Calling of the Disciples? (One searches for the figure of Christ.) Some would argue that this is because the artist's attitude to his subject was ambivalent. I would argue that the *optic* of all the visual means he was using with such care, pre-empted the possibility of depicting manual work, as the main subject of a painting, in any but a mythological or symbolic way.

The crisis provoked by those who tried to extend the area of experience to which painting might be open — and by the end of the century this also included the Impressionists — continued into the 20th century. But its terms were reversed. The tradition was indeed dismantled. Yet, except for the introduction of the Unconscious, the area of experience from which most European artists drew remained surprisingly unchanged. Consequently, most of the serious art of the period dealt either with the experience of various kinds of isolation, or with the narrow experience of painting itself. The latter produced painting about painting, abstract art.

One of the reasons why the potential freedom gained by the dismantling of the tradition was not used, may be to do with the way painters were still trained. In the academies and art schools they first learnt those very conventions which were being dismantled. This was because no other professional body of knowledge existed to be taught. And this is still, more or less, true today. No other professionalism exists.

Recently, corporate capitalism, having grounds to believe itself triumphant, has begun to adopt abstract art. And the adoption is proving easy. Diagrams of aesthetic power lend themselves to becoming emblems of economic power. In the process almost all lived experience has been eliminated from the image. Thus, the extreme of abstract art demonstrates, as an epilogue, the original problematic of professional art: an art in reality concerned with a selective, very reduced area of experience, which nevertheless claims to be universal.

Something like this overview of traditional art (and the overview is of course only partial, there are other things to be said on other occasions) may help us to answer the questions about primitive art.

The first primitive artists appeared during the second half of the 19th century. They appeared after professional art had first questioned its own conventional purposes. The notorious Salon des Refusés was held in 1863. This exhibition was not of course the reason for their appearance. What helped to make their appearance possible were universal primary education (paper, pencils, ink), the spread of popular journalism, a new geographical mobility due to the railways, the stimulus of clearer class consciousness. Perhaps also the example of the *bohemian* professional artist had its effect. The bohemian chose to live in a way which defied normal class divisions, and his life-style, if not his work, tended to suggest that art could come from any class.

Among the first were the Douanier Rousseau (1844-1910) and the Facteur Cheval (1836-1924). These men, when their art eventually became known, were nevertheless designated by their other work — the Customs-Man-Rousseau, the Postman-Cheval. This makes it clear — as does also the term *Sunday painter* — that their "art" is an eccentricity. They were treated as cultural "sports", not because of their class origin, but because they refused, or were ignorant of, the fact that all artistic expression has traditionally to undergo a class transformation. In this way they were quite

67

distinct from *amateurs* — most, but not all of whom, came from the cultured classes; amateurs, by definition, followed, with less rigour, the example of the professionals.

The primitive begins alone; he inherits no practice. Because of this the term *primitive* may appear at first to be justified. He does not use the pictorial grammar of the tradition — hence he is ungrammatical. He has not learnt the technical skills which have evolved with the conventions — hence he is clumsy. When he discovers on his own a solution to a pictorial problem, he often uses it many times — hence he is naïve. But then one has to ask: why does he refuse the tradition? And the answer is only partly that he was born far away from that tradition. The effort necessary to begin painting or sculpting, in the social context in which he finds himself, is so great that it could well include visiting the museums. But it never does, at least at the beginning. Why? Because he knows already that his own lived experience which is forcing him to make art has no place in that tradition. How does he know this without having visited the museums? He knows it because his whole experience is one of being excluded from the exercise of power in his society, and he realises from the compulsion he now feels, that art too has a kind of power. The will of primitives derives from faith in their own experience and a profound scepticism about society as they have found it. This is true even of such an amiable artist as Grandma Moses.

I hope I have now made clearer why the "clumsiness" of primitive art is the precondition of its eloquence. What it is saying could never be said with any ready-made skills. For what it is saying was never meant, according to the cultural class system, to be said.

1976

Millet and the Peasant

Jean-François Millet died in 1875. After his death and until recently, a number of his paintings, particularly *The Angelus, The Sower* and *The Gleaners,* were among the best-known painted images in the world. I doubt whether even today there is a peasant family in France who do not know all three pictures through engravings, cards, ornaments or plates. *The Sower* became both the trademark for a US bank and a symbol of revolution in Peking and Cuba.

As Millet's popular reputation spread, his "critical" reputation declined. Originally, however, his work had been admired by Seurat, Pissarro, Cézanne, Van Gogh. Commentators talk today of Millet becoming a posthumous victim of his own popularity. The questions raised by Millet's art are more far-reaching and more disturbing than this suggests. A whole tradition of culture is in question.

In 1862 Millet painted *Winter with Crows*. It is nothing but a sky, a distant copse, and a vast deserted plain of inert earth, on which have been left a wooden plough and a harrow. Crows comb the ground whilst waiting, as they will all winter. A painting of the starkest simplicity. Scarcely a landscape but a portrait in November of a plain. The horizontality of that plain claims everything. To cultivate its soil is a continual struggle to encourage the vertical. This struggle, the painting declares, is back-breaking.

Millet's images were reproduced on such a wide scale because they were unique: no other European painter had treated rural labour as the central theme of his art. His life's work was to introduce a new subject into an old tradition, to force a language to speak of what it had ignored. The language was that of oil painting; the subject was the peasant as individual *subject.*

Some may want to contest this claim by citing Breughel

and Courbet. In Breughel, peasants form a large part of the crowd which is mankind: Breughel's subject is a collectivity of which the peasantry as a whole is only a part; no man has yet been condemned in perpetuity to solitary individuality and all men are equal before the last judgment; social station is secondary.

Courbet may have painted *The Stonebreakers* in 1850 under Millet's influence (Millet's first Salon "success" was with *The Winnower,* exhibited in 1848). But essentially Courbet's imagination was sensuous, concerned with the sources of sense experience rather than with the subject of them. As an artist of peasant origin, Courbet's achievement was to introduce into painting a new kind of substantiality, perceived according to senses developed by habits different from those of the urban bourgeois. The fish as caught by a fisherman, the dog as chosen by a hunter, the trees and snow as what a familiar path leads through, a funeral as a regular village meeting. What Courbet was weakest at painting was the human eye. In his many portraits, the eyes (as distinct from the lids and eye sockets) are almost interchangeable. He refused any insight inwards. This explains why the peasant *as subject* could not be his theme.

Among Millet's paintings are the following experiences; scything, sheep shearing, splitting wood, potato lifting, digging, shepherding, manuring, pruning. Most of the jobs are seasonal, and so their experience includes the experience of a particular kind of weather. The sky behind the couple in *The Angelus* (1859) is typical of the stillness of early autumn. If a shepherd is out at night with his sheep, hoar frost on their wool is as likely as moonlight. Because Millet was inevitably addressing an urban and privileged public, he chose to depict moments which emphasise the harshness of the peasant experience — often a moment of exhaustion.

Job and, once again, season determine the expression of this exhaustion. The man with a hoe leans, looking unseeing up at the sky, straightening his back. The haymakers lie prostrate in the shade. The man in the vineyard sits huddled on the parched earth surrounded by green leaves.

So strong was Millet's ambition to introduce previously unpainted experience that sometimes he set himself an impossible task. A woman dropping seed potatoes into a hole scooped out by her husband (the potatoes in mid-air!) may be filmable, but is scarcely paintable. At other times his originality is impressive. A drawing of cattle with a shepherd dissolving into darkness, the scene absorbing dusk like dunked bread absorbs coffee. A painting of earth and bushes, just discernible by starlight, as blanketed masses.

The universe sleeps
And its gigantic ear
Full of ticks
That are stars
Is now laid on its paw —
(Mayakovsky)

Such experiences had never been painted before — not even by Van de Neer, whose night scenes were still delineated as if they were day scenes. (Millet's love of night and half-light is something to come back to.)

What provoked Millet to choose such new subject matter? It is not enough to say that he painted peasants because he came from a peasant family in Normandy and, when young, had worked on the land. Any more than it is correct to assume that the "biblical" solemnity of his work was the result of his own religious faith. In fact, he was an agnostic.

In 1847, when he was 33, he painted a small picture entitled *Return from the Fields* which shows three nymphs —

seen somewhat in the manner of Fragonard — playing on a barrow of hay. A light rustic idyll for a bedroom or private library. It was one year later that he painted coarsely the taut figure of *The Winnower* in the dark of a barn where dust rises from his basket, like the dust of white brass, a sign of the energy with which his whole body is shaking the grain. And two years later, *The Sower* striding downhill, broadcasting his grain, a figure symbolising the bread of life, whose silhouette and inexorability are reminiscent of the figure of death. What inspired the change in Millet's painting after 1847 was the revolution of 1848.

His view of history was too passive and too pessimistic to allow him any strong political convictions. Yet the years of 1848 to 1851, the hopes they raised and suppressed, established for him, as for many others, the claim of democracy: not so much in a parliamentary sense, as in the sense of the rights of man being universally applicable. The artistic style which accompanied this modern claim was realism: realism because it revealed hidden social conditions, realism because (it was believed) all could recognise what it revealed.

After 1847, Millet devoted the remaining 27 years of his life to revealing the living conditions of the French peasantry. Two thirds of the population were peasants. The revolution of 1789 had freed the peasantry from feudal servitude, but by the middle of the 19th century they had become victims of the "free exchange" of capital. The annual interest the French peasantry had to pay on mortgages and loans was equal to that paid on the entire annual national debt of Britain, the richest country in the world. Most of the public who went to look at paintings in the Salon were ignorant of the penury which existed in the countryside, and one of Millet's conscious aims was "to

72

disturb them in their contentment and leisure.''

His choice of subject also involved nostalgia. In a double sense. Like many who leave their village, he was nostalgic about his own village childhood. For 20 years he worked on a canvas showing the road to the hamlet where he was born, finishing it two years before he died. Intensely green, sewn

together, the shadows as substantially dark as the lights are substantially light, this landscape is like a garment he once wore (*The Hameau Cousin*). And there is a pastel of a well in front of a house with geese and chickens and a woman, which made an extraordinary impression on me when I first looked at it. It is drawn realistically and yet I saw it as the site of every fairy story which begins with an old woman's cottage. I saw it as a hundred times familiar, although I knew I had not seen it before; the ''memory'' was inexplicably in the drawing itself. Later I discovered in

Robert L. Herbert's exemplary catalogue to the 1976 exhibition that this scene was what was visible in front of the house where Millet was born, and that consciously or unconsciously the artist had enlarged the proportions of the well by two thirds so that they coincided with his childhood perception.

Millet's nostalgia, however, was not confined to the personal. It permeated his view of history. He was sceptical of the Progress being proclaimed on every side and saw it, rather, as an eventual threat to human dignity. Yet unlike William Morris and other romantic medievalists, he did not sentimentalise the village. Most of what he knew about peasants was that they were reduced to a brutal existence, especially the men. And, however conservative and negative his overall perspective may have been, he sensed, it seems to me, two things which, at the time, few others foresaw: that the poverty of the city and its suburbs; and that the market created by industrialisation, to which the peasantry was being sacrificed, might one day entail the loss of all sense of history. This is why for Millet the peasant came to stand for man, and why he saw his paintings as having an historic function.

The reactions to his paintings were as complex as Millet's own feelings. Straightaway he was labelled a socialist revolutionary. With enthusiasm by the left. With outraged horror by the centre and right. The latter were able to say about his *painted* peasants what they feared but dared not say about the real ones, who were still working on the land, or the five million who were drifting landless towards the cities: *they look like murderers, they are cretins, they are beasts not men, they are degenerate.* Having said these things, they accused Millet of inventing such figures.

Towards the end of the century, when the economic and

social stability of capitalism was more assured, his paintings offered other meanings. Reproduced by the church and commerce, they reached the countryside. The pride with which a class first sees itself recognisably depicted in a permanent art is full of pleasure, even if the art is flawed and the truth harsh. The depiction gives an historic resonance to their lives. A pride which was, before, an obstinate refusal of shame, becomes an affirmation.

Meanwhile the original Millets were being bought by old millionaires in America who wanted to re-believe that the best things in life are simple and free.

And so how are we to judge this advent of a new subject into an old art? It is necessary to emphasise how conscious Millet was of the tradition he inherited. He worked slowly from drawings, often returning to the same motif. Having chosen the peasant as subject, his life's effort was to do him justice by investing him with dignity and permanence. And this meant joining him to the tradition of Giorgione, Michelangelo, the Dutch 17th century, Poussin, Chardin.

Look at his art chronologically and you see the peasant emerging, quite literally, from the shadows. The shadows are the corner traditionally reserved for genre painting — the scene of low life (tavern, servant's quarters), glimpsed in passing, indulgently even enviously, by the traveller on the high road where there is space and light. *The Winnower* is still in the genre corner, but enlarged. *The Sower* is a phantom figure, oddly uncompleted as a painting, striding forward to claim a place. Up to about 1856 Millet produced other genre paintings — shepherd girls in the shade of trees, a woman churning butter, a cooper in his workshop. But already in 1853, in *Going to Work,* the couple leaving home for the day's work on the plain — they are modelled on Masaccio's *Adam and Eve* — have moved to the forefront and become the centre of the world assumed by the painting. And from now on, this is true in all of Millet's major works which include figures. Far from presenting these figures as something marginal seen in passing, he does his utmost to make them central and monumental. And all these paintings — in differing degrees — fail.

They fail because no unity is established between figures and surroundings. The monumentality of the figures refuses the painting. And vice versa. As a result the cut-out figures look rigid and theatrical. The moment lasts too long. By contrast, the same figures in equivalent drawings or etchings are alive and belong to the moment of drawing which includes all their surroundings. For example, the etching of *Going to Work,* made ten years after the painting, is a very great work, comparable with the finest etching by Rembrandt.

What prevented Millet achieving his aim as a painter? There are two conventional fallback answers. Most 19th century sketches were better than finished works. A doubtful art-historical generalisation. Or: Millet was not a born painter!

I believe that he failed because the language of traditional oil painting could not accommodate the subject he brought with him. One can explain this ideologically. The peasant's interest in the *land* expressed through his actions, is incommensurate with scenic landscape. Most (not all) European landscape painting was addressed to a visitor from the city, later called a tourist; the landscape is *his* view, the splendour of it is *his* reward. Its paradigm is one of those painted orientation tables which name the visible landmarks. Imagine a peasant suddenly appearing at work between the table and the view, and the social/human contradiction becomes obvious.

The history of forms reveals the same incompatibility.

There were various iconographic formulae for integrating figures and landscape. Distant figures like notes of colour. Portraits to which the landscape is a background. Mythological figures, goddesses and so on, with which nature interweaves to "dance to the music of time." Dramatic figures, whose passions nature reflects and illustrates. The visitor or solitary onlooker who surveys the scene, an *alter ego* for the spectator himself. But there was no formula for representing the close, harsh, patient physicality of a peasant's labour *on,* instead of *in front of,* the land. And to invent one would mean destroying the traditional language for depicting scenic landscape.

In fact, only a few years after Millet's death, this is exactly what Van Gogh tried to do. Millet was his chosen master, both spiritually and artistically. He made dozens of paintings copied closely from engravings from Millet. In these paintings Van Gogh united the working figure with his surroundings by the gestures and energy of his own brush strokes. Such energy was released by his intense sense of empathy with the subject.

But the result was to turn the painting into a personal vision, which was characterised by its "handwriting." The witness had become more important than his testimony. The way was open to expressionism and, later, to abstract expressionism, and the final destruction of painting as a language of supposedly objective reference. Thus Millet's failure and setback may be seen as an historic turning point. The claim of universal democracy was inadmissible for oil painting. And the consequent crisis of meaning forced most painting to become autobiographical.

Why not inadmissible, too, for drawing and graphic work? A drawing records a visual experience. An oil painting, because of its uniquely large range of tones, textures and colours, pretends to reproduce the visible. The difference is very great. The virtuoso performance of the oil painting assembles all aspects of the visible to conduct them to a single point: the point of view of the empirical onlooker. And it insists that such a view constitutes visibility itself. Graphic work, with its limited means, is more modest; it only claims a single aspect of visual experience, and therefore is adaptable to different uses.

Millet's increasing use of pastel towards the end of his life, his love of half-light in which visibility itself becomes problematic, his fascination with night scenes, suggest that intuitively he may have tried to resist the demand of the privileged onlooker for the world arranged as his view. It would have been in line with Millet's sympathies, for did not the inadmissibility of the peasant as a subject into the European tradition of painting, prefigure exactly the absolute conflict of interests which exists today between first and third worlds? If this is the case, Millet's life's work shows how nothing can resolve this conflict unless the hierarchy of our social and cultural values is radically altered.

1976

Seker Ahmet and the Forest

The painting measures 138 × 177 centimetres. Fairly large. It was painted towards the end of the last century in Istanbul. The artist, Seker Ahmet Pasa (1841-1907), worked for a period in Paris, where he was strongly influenced by Courbet and the Barbizon school, and returned to Turkey to become one of the two leading painters whose work introduced a European optic into Turkish art. The painting is entitled *Woodcutter in the Forest.*

As soon as I looked at it, it began to interest and haunt me. Not really because it might introduce me to the work of a painter I did not know, but in itself, this canvas. After going back to the museum in Besiktas, several times to look

79

at the picture. I began to understand more fully why it interested me. Why it haunts me I only understood later.

The colours, the paint texture, the tonality of the painting, are very reminiscent of a Rousseau, a Courbet, a Diaz. With half a glance you read it like a pre-impressionist European landscape, another look at a forest. Yet there is a gravity in it which checks you. And then this gravity turns out to be a peculiarity. There is something deeply but subtly strange about the perspective, about the relationship between the woodcutter with his mule and the far edge of the forest in the top right-hand corner. You see that it is the *far* edge, and, at the same time, that third distant tree (a beech?) appears nearer than anything else in the painting. It simultaneously withdraws and approaches.

There are reasons for this. I'm not creating mysteries. There is the size of the beech trunk (supposed to be 100 or 150 yards away) relative to the size of the man. The beech leaves are as large as the leaves on the nearest tree. The light falling on the beech trunk brings it forward, whereas the two other dark trunks are both leaning away from you. Most important of all — because every convincing painting makes a spatial system of its own — there is the strange diagonal line of the edge of the receding brushwood which begins on this side of the bridge and extends up to the edge of the forest. This line, this edge, "concurs" with the third dimensional space, and yet stays on the surface of the painting. It creates a spatial ambiguity. Block it out for a moment, and you will see the beech move back somewhat into the distance.

Each of these things is, academically speaking, a mistake. More than that, they contradict for any viewer, academically minded or not, the logic of the language with which everything else is painted. In a work of art such inconsistency is not usually impressive — it leads to a lack of conviction. The more so when it is unintentional. And the rest of Seker Ahmet's work, though it does suggest that he may have been unusually spiritually illuminated, does not suggest that he would ever consciously question the visual language he had learnt so hard in Paris.

So I was faced with two questions. Why was the painting so convincing or, if you wish, about *what* was it so convincing? And the second question: how did Seker Ahmet come to paint it in the way he did?

If the far beech tree between the edge of the forest and the far side of the clearing is nearer than anything else in the painting, then you are looking *into* the forest from its far edge, and from this point of view the woodcutter and his mule are what is farthest away. Yet we also see him *in* the forest, dwarfed by the huge trees, about to cart across the clearing his load of wood. Why does such a double vision have so precise an authority about it?

Its precision is existential. It accords with the experience of forest. The attraction and the terror of the forest is that you see yourself *in* it as Jonah was in the whale's belly. Although it has limits, it is closed around you. Now this experience, which is that of anybody familiar with forests, depends upon your seeing yourself in double vision. You make your way through the forest and, simultaneously, you see yourself, as from the outside, swallowed by the forest. What gives this painting its peculiar authority is its faithfulness to the experience of the figure of the woodcutter.

When I wrote about Millet, I suggested that one of the enormous difficulties he faced was that of painting the peasant working on the land instead of *in front of it*. This was because Millet inherited a language of landscape painting which had been developed to speak about the traveller's view of a landscape. The problem is epitomised by the horizon. The traveller/spectator looks towards the horizon:

for the working peasant bent over the land, the horizon is either invisible or is the totally surrounding edge of the sky from which the weather comes. The language of European landscape could not give expression to such an experience.

Later the same year an exhibition of Chinese peasant paintings from the Hu county came to London. Out of nearly 80 paintings showing peasants working out of doors only 16 showed the sky or an horizon. Although the paintings, painted by peasants themselves (under some supervision), were far more matter-of-fact than traditional Chinese landscape painting, the latter offered them a relativity of perspective which could, at least partly, accommodate the spatial experience of peasants working on the land. Some of the pictures failed, offering only a helicopter overview which incorporated, graphically, the view of an overseer! Others succeeded. For example, something true of the experience of minding goats, the least domesticated of the domesticated animals, who wander everywhere and need continual *surveillance,* is present in Pai Tien-hsueh's gouache.

This is why Seker Ahmet's painting of the forest so interested me. There was already a place prepared in my mind for its surprise.

How did he come to paint it in the way he did? At one level the question is unanswerable and we shall never know. But it is possible to guess at the depth at which his imagination was working to reconcile two opposed ways of seeing. Before the influence of European painting, the Turkish pictorial tradition was one of book illustrations and miniatures. Many of the latter were Persian. The traditional pictorial language was one of signs and embellishment: its space was spiritual not physical. Light was not something which crossed emptiness but was, rather, an emanation.

For Seker Ahmet the decision to change from one

82

language to another must have been far more problematic than might at first appear to us. It was not just a question of observing what he saw in the Louvre, for what was involved was a whole view of the world, man and history. He was not changing a technique, but an ontology. Spatial perspective is closely connected with the question of time. The fully articulated system of European landscape perspective such as one finds in Poussin, Claude Lorraine, Ruysdael, Hobbema, only preceded by a decade or two Vico's invention of modern history. The path which led away and vanished on the horizon was also that of unilinear time.

Thus there is a close parallel between pictorial representations of space and the ways in which stories are told. The novel, as Lukacs pointed out in *Theory of the Novel,* was born of a yearning for what now lay beyond the horizon:it was the art-form of a sense of homelessness. With this homelessness came an openness of choice (most novels are primarily about choices) such as man had never experienced before. Earlier narrative forms are more two-dimensional, but not for that reason less real. Instead of choice, there is pressing necessity. Each event is unavoidable as soon as it is present. The only choices are about treating, coming to terms with, *what is there.* One can talk about immediacy, but since all events narrated in this way are immediate, the term changes its meaning. Events come into being like the genie of Aladdin's lamp. They are equally irrefutable, expected and unexpected.

In telling the story of the woodcutter, Seker Ahmet found himself facing the forest like the woodcutter. Neither Courbet in painting nor Turgenev in literature (I think of those two because they are contemporary and they both loved forests) could possibly have faced it in the same way. They would both have *placed* the forest, relating it to the world which was not the forest. Or to say the same thing differently, they would have seen the forest as a *scene* in which significant things took place: a deer dying or a hunter thinking about love.

Seker Ahmet, on the other hand, faced the forest as a thing taking place in itself, as a presence that was so pressing that he could not, as he had learnt to do in Paris, maintain his distance from it. This, I think, is what caused the disjuncture to open between the two traditions: the disjuncture in which this forest painting has its being.

Yet having answered its questions, why should it go on haunting me? Months later, back in Europe, I began to see why. I was reading Heidegger's "Conversation on a country path about thinking," in his *Discourse on Thinking:*

TEACHER: . . . what lets the horizon be what it is, has not yet been encountered at all.

SCIENTIST: What do you have in mind in this statement?

TEACHER: We say that we look into the horizon. Therefore the field of vision is something open, but its openness is not due to our looking.

SCHOLAR: Likewise we do not place the appearance of objects, which the view within a field of vision offers us, into this openness . . .

SCIENTIST: . . . rather that comes out of this to meet us . . .

SCIENTIST: Then thinking would be coming-into-the-nearness of distance.

SCHOLAR: That is a daring definition of its nature, which we have chanced upon.

SCIENTIST: I only brought together that which we have named, but without representing anything to myself.

TEACHER: Yet you have thought something.

SCIENTIST: Or, really, waited for something without knowing for what.

This quotation belongs to the years 1944-45 when Heidegger, in his mid-fifties, was seeking more metaphoric and vernacular ways of conveying the significance of the fundamental philosophical question which he had raised in *Being and Time* (1927). The sense of thought as the "coming-into-the-nearness of distance" is central to that question. (For those unfamiliar with Heidegger's life's work, I would recommend George Steiner's admirable small paperback in the Fontana Modern Masters series.)

Had Heidegger known this Turkish painting I think he would have been tempted to write about it. His father worked as a carpenter and he was born in the Black Forest. Continually he uses the forest as a symbol of reality. The task of philosophy is to find the *Weg,* the woodcutter's path, through the forest. The path may lead to the *Lichtung,* the clearing whose very space, open to light and vision, is the most surprising thing about existence, and is the very condition of Being. "The clearing is the open for everything that is present and absent."

Heidegger would undoubtedly have given weight to the fact that Seker Ahmet had not been brought up in any school of European reasoning. His own philosophical starting point was that post-Socratic European thought from Plato to Kant had only answered the comparatively easy questions. The fundamental question, opened by surprise at the very fact of being, had been closed. An artist from a different culture might feel the question was still open.

Seker Ahmet's painting is about the "coming-into-the-nearness of distance." I can think of no other painting of which this is so explicitly true. (Implicitly the later work of Cézanne is very close to Heidegger's vision, which is perhaps why Merleau-Ponty, a follower of Heidegger, understood him so deeply.) In the "coming-into-the-nearness of distance" there is a reciprocal movement.

85

Thought approaches the distant; but the distant also approaches thought.

For Heidegger the present, the now, is not a measurable unit of time, but the result of presence, of the existent actively presenting itself. In his attempt to bend language to describe this, he turns the word presence into a verb: *presencing*. Tentatively, Novalis prefigured this when he wrote: ''Perceptibility is a kind of attentiveness.''

The woodcutter and his mule are stepping forward. Yet the painting renders them almost static. They are scarcely moving. What is moving — and this is so surprising that one senses it without at first being able to realise it — is the forest. The forest with its presence is moving in the opposite direction to the woodcutter — ie, forward towards us and leftwards. ''Presence means: the constant abiding that approaches man, reaches him, is extended to him.'' It is unimportant here how obscure or meaningful one judges Heidegger's contribution to modern thought to be. In relation to this painting his words become apposite and transparent. They reveal the painting, and they reveal why it is haunting. The painting confirms them.

Such a coincidence between a painting of a local 19th century Turkish painter who studied in Paris and the thoughts of a German professor whom some consider the most important European philosopher of the 20th century, is an example of how, at this stage of world history, there are truths which can only be uncovered or, as Heidegger would say, *unconcealed*, in the folds between cultures and epochs.

1979

Lowry and the Industrial North

Lowry was born in a Manchester suburb in 1887. He was a vague child. He never passed any exams. He went to art school because nobody was very convinced that he could do anything else. At the age of about thirty he began to paint the industrial scene around him: he began to produce what would now be recognizable Lowrys. He continued for twenty years with scant recognition or success. Then a London dealer saw some of his paintings by chance when he went to a framer's. He inquired about the artist. A London exhibition was arranged — it was now 1938, and Lowry began slowly to acquire a national reputation. At first it was other artists who most appreciated his work. The public gradually followed. From 1945 onwards he began to receive official honours — honorary degrees, Royal Academician, freedom of the City of Salford. None of this has changed him in any way. He still lives on the outskirts of Manchester: modest, eccentric, comic, lonely.

"You know, I've never been able to get used to the fact that I'm alive! The whole thing frightens me. It's been like that from my earliest days. It's too big you know — I mean life, sir."*

In 1964 the Hallé Orchestra gave a special concert in honour of Lowry's seventy-fifth birthday: a number of artists, including Henry Moore, Victor Pasmore and Ivon Hitchens, contributed to an honorary exhibition: and Sir Kenneth Clark wrote an appreciation. In it, Clark compares Lowry to Wordworth's "Leech Gatherer":

* This quotation is from Mervyn Levy's *L. S. Lowry* (London: Studio Vista, 1961). Levy establishes the character of the artist very well, but his interpretation of the works is vulgar.

"Our leech gatherer has continued to scrutinise his small black figures in their milky pool of atmosphere, isolating and combining them with a loving sense of their human qualities . . . All those black people walking to and fro are as anonymous, as inidividual, as purposeless and as directed as the stream of real people who pass before our eyes in the square of an industrial town." (Kenneth Clark, *A tribute to L. S. Lowry,* Monks Hall Museum, Eccles, 1964.)

Edwin Mullins, who wrote the introduction to the catalogue of Lowry's retrospective exhibition at the Tate in 1966, makes the point that Lowry is primarily interested in "the battle of life."

"It is a battle engaged between undignified pea-brained homunculi who pour out of a mill after a day's work, or congregate round a street fight, pace a railway platform, whoop it up on V.E. Day, watch a regatta or football match, take a pram and an idiotic dog for a walk along the promenade." (*L. S. Lowry,* Arts Council Catalogue, 1966.)

These quotations reveal the submerged patronage found in nearly all critical comment on Lowry's work. This tendency to patronize is a form of self-defence: defence not so much against the artist as against the subject-matter of his work. It is hard to reconcile a life devoted to aesthetic expositions with the streets and houses and front doors of those who live in Bury, Rochdale, Burnley or Salford.

Lowry has been compared with Chaplin, Breughel and the Douanier Rousseau. The curious mood of his work has been analysed, sometimes with considerable subtlety. His technique has been explained and it has been pointed out that technically he is a highly sophisticated artist. Many stories are told about his behaviour and conversation. He is indeed an original, dignified man for whom one can feel deeply.

I might add stories of my own, but there is something more important to say. The extraordinary fact is that nobody, faced with Lowry's pictures whose subject-matter is nearly always social, ever discusses the social or historical meaning of his art. Instead it is treated as though it dealt with the view out of the window of a Pullman train on its non-stop journey to London, where everything is believed to be very different. His subjects, if they have to be considered at all in relation to what actually exists, are considered as local exotica.

I don't want to exaggerate the meaning of Lowry's work or give it a historical load which is too heavy for it. The range of his work is small. It does not belong to the mainstream of twentieth-century art, which is concerned in one way or another with interpreting new relationships between man and nature. It is a spontaneous (as opposed to a consciously self-developing) art. It is static, local and subjectively repetitive. But is is consistent within itself, courageous, obstinate, unique, and the phenomenon of its creation and appreciation *is* significant.

Perhaps I should emphasize here that this significance must be considered separately from, though not necessarily in opposition to, Lowry's conscious intentions. He says he doesn't know why he paints his pictures. They come to him.

"I started as I often do, with nothing particular in mind; things just happen — they grow from nothing. When I had painted the figure of the woman on the left, walking away, I got stuck. I just couldn't think what to do next. Then a young lady friend of mine came to the rescue. 'Why don't you paint another figure walking towards you,' she suggested. 'Shall I paint the same woman turned around?' I asked. 'Yes,' she said, 'that would be a very good idea.' 'All right,' I replied, 'but what can I call the picture?' 'Why not

call it *The Same Woman Coming Back?'* she said. And I did!''
(Mervyn Levy, *L. S. Lowry, op. cit.*)

Even allowing for the simplification Lowry makes in
telling this story, it is clear that he works intuitively, without
fixed aims. His aim is only to finish the picture. Any wider
significance his work may have is the result of a certain
coincidence between his own private half-hidden
motivations and the nature of the outside world which he
uses as raw material and to which he delivers back his
finished pictures. On a certain level, he himself is probably
aware of this coincidence: it is probably the substance of his
conviction that what he has to say as an artist is, in some
mysterious way, relevant. But this is very far from implying
that he consciously intends the meaning which his pictures
acquire.

What is this meaning? I have already suggested that its
basis is social. Let us now try to place Lowry's pictures
within a context. First, they are very specifically English.
They could be about nowhere else. Nowhere else are there
comparable industrial landscapes. The light, which is not
natural but which was manufactured in the nineteenth
century, is unique. Only in the Midlands and North of
England do people live — to use Sir Kenneth Clark's
euphemism — in such a milky pool.

The character of the figures and crowds is also specially
English. The industrial revolution has isolated them and
uprooted them. Their home-made ideology, except when
they are led and organized by revolutionaries, is a kind of
ironic stoicism. Nowhere else do crowds look so
simultaneously *civic* and *deprived.* They appear to have as
little to lose as a mob: and yet they are not a mob. They
know each other, recognize each other, exchange help and
jokes — they are not, as is sometimes said, like lost souls in

limbo; they are fellow-travellers through a life which is impervious to most of their choices.

All this might seem at first to date Lowry's paintings. One might suppose that they are more to do with the nineteenth century than with today when there are television aerials on the houses, cars in the back streets, hairdressers for mill girls, and a Labour government.

Yet, in order to place Lowry's work within an historical as well as geographical context, we must distinguish rather carefully between different elements in it. Most of Lowry's paintings are synthetic, insofar as they are constructed from his observation and memory of different incidents and places. Only a few represent specific scenes. If, however, one goes to the mill towns, to the potteries, to Manchester, to Barrow-in-Furness, to Liverpool, one finds countless streets, skylines, doorsteps, bus stops, squares, churches, homes, which look like those depicted by Lowry, and have never been depicted by anybody else. His paintings are no more dated than certain English cities and towns.

If one looks more carefully at the pictures one notices that the figures, even in the most recent ones, are wearing clothes which belong, at the latest, to the 1920s or early 1930s: that is to say to the period when Lowry first determined to paint the area where he had been brought up and where he was going to spend the rest of his life. Similarly, there are very few cars or modern buildings to be seen. He says that he hates change. And his pictures, both in detail, as cited above, and in general spirit, suggest an essential changelessness. (One sees this in a different way in his deserted landscapes and seascapes of endlessly repeating hills or waves). The bustle of the crowds, the walk to the sea and back, the fight, the accident, the crippling of others, changes nothing. In certain canvases this sense of unchanging time becomes an almost metaphysical sense of eternity.

Thus we can summarize: Lowry's paintings correspond in many respects to existing places; certain details belong to the past; the artist's vision exaggerates a feeling of changelessness. The three elements combine together to create an atmosphere of dramatic obsolescence. Stylistic considerations apart, there is in fact no question of these pictures belonging to the spirit of the nineteenth century. The notion of progress — however it is applied — is foreign to them. Their virtues are stoic: their logic is one of decline.

These paintings are about what has been happening to the British economy since 1918, and their logic implies the collapse still to come. This is what has happened to the "workshop of the world." Here is the recurring so-called production crisis; the obsolete industrial plants; the inadequacy of unchanged transport systems and overstrained power supplies; the failure of education to keep pace with technological advance; the ineffectiveness of national planning; the lack of capital investment at home and the disastrous reliance on colonial and neo-colonial overseas investments; the shift of power from industrial capital to international finance capital; the essential agreements within the two-party system blocking every initiative towards political independence and thus economic viability.

The argument is not so far-fetched as it may seem if one pauses to consider the circumstances in which the pictures have been painted. Lowry has happened to live and work in an area where the truth of our economic decline has been far less disguised than elsewhere. His art is partly subjective, but what he has seen around him has confirmed, and perhaps even helped to sustain and create, his subjective tendencies. In the 1920s, Lancashire was a depressed area. (One tends to forget that before the depression of the 1930s,

92

there were never less than one million unemployed.) What the 1930s were like has been described many times. Yet the relevance of their desolation to Lowry is seldom mentioned. Here Orwell, in *The Road to Wigan Pier,* is virtually describing a painting by Lowry.

"I remember a winter afternoon in the dreadful environs of Wigan. All round was the lunar landscape of slag heaps, and to the north, through the passes, as it were, between the mountains of slag, you could see factory chimneys sending out their plumes of smoke. The canal path was a mixture of cinders and frozen mud, criss-crossed by the imprints of innumerable clogs, and all round, as far as the slag heaps in the distance, stretched the 'flashes' — pools of stagnant water that had seeped into the hollows caused by the subsidence of ancient pits. It was horribly cold. The 'flashes' were covered with ice the colour of raw umber, the bargemen were muffled to the eyes in sacks, the lock gates wore tears of ice. It seemed a world from which vegetation had been banished; nothing existed except smoke, shale, ice, mud, ashes, and foul water."

The poverty of the 1930s has passed. But in many parts of the north-west today there is a sense of profound exhaustion. There is nothing Spenglerian about this: it is the result of the scale of what has to be destroyed before anything can be renewed. Town-planners, investors, educationalists know it. I quote from the government's North-West Study, published in 1965:

"Slums, general obsolescence, dereliction and neglect all add up to a formidable problem of environmental renewal extending over a wide area of the region. It is plain that this problem cannot be disposed of in a few years and the question which arises is whether it is feasible to break the back of it in, say, ten to 15 years or whether the turn of another century will find Lancashire still struggling under the grim heritage of the industrial revolution.''

In a different way many of the voters know it too. They have always voted Labour, believing in an alternative plan. Today they see Wilson thirty-five years later performing the same role as Ramsay MacDonald and abandoning any possibility of an alternative.

Historians of the future will cite Lowry's work as both expressing and illustrating the industrial and economic decline of British capitalism since the First World War. But of course he is not simply that, as described in those remote terms. He is an artist concerned with loneliness, with a certain humour — somewhat like Samuel Beckett's: the humour found in the contemplation of time passing without meaning. He is an artist who has uniquely found a way of painting the character of hand-me-down clothes, the sensation of damp rising from the ground, the effect of smog on the texture of the surfaces exposed to it, the strange closing of distance which smoke and mist bring about so that each person carries with him his own small parcel of visibility, which constitutes his world.

''My three most cherished records,'' says Lowry, ''are the fact that I've never been abroad, never had a telephone and never owned a motor-car.'' He is a man strongly attached to where he found himself. Everything in his work is informed by the character of a specific place and period.

I have tried to define that character. If Lowry were a greater artist, there would be more of himself in his work. (His ''naïvety'' is probably an excuse for hiding his own experience.) It would then be far less possible to localize his work, either geographically or historically: emotions are always more general than circumstances. As it is, given his inhibitions as an artist, he intuitively chose correctly. He chose to paint the historic.

1966

Ralph Fasanella and the Experience of the City

Only somebody who has lived in the streets of a city, suffering some kind of misery, can be aware of what the paving stones, the doorways, the bricks, the windows signify. At street level — outside a vehicle — all modern cities are violent and tragic. The violence of which the media and police reports speak so much, is partly a reflection of this more continuous but unregarded and older violence. The violence of the daily necessity of the streets — of which the traffic is a symbolic expression — to obliterate (run over) even the recent history of those who have lived and live in them.

Ralph Fasanella was born in Manhattan of Southern Italian immigrant parents in 1914. His father, who earned such a living as they had selling ice from a cart, came from Bari: a town I can never forget — though I was only there once — a town that is continually emptying itself.

Initially Fasanella's paintings of Manhattan do not appear in the least tragic. And this is the first way in which they are accurate. Because tragedy, to be felt as such, requires a temporary exemption from daily life — a compassionate leave — which the modern city does not grant.

His paintings are accurate in many ways. There's the typical sky of New York, very high and distant and yet its light indistinguishable from that reflected off the waters from the Bay, the Hudson and the East River, and all the light, however bright, as if filtered through gauze. The colours of the small shop fronts and other poor buildings like those of faded cheap cotton fabrics. Or the specific way in which the density of the working population makes itself felt there. The island of Manhattan is a gigantic metaphoric model of the compression of an immigrant ship that has moored and never left. Every apartment is like a berth. Every square metre of street is deck. The skyscraping offices are the bridge. Harlem and other areas are the hold.

There are certain pictorial reasons why Fasanella achieves such a remarkable likeness. (Though these don't explain the uniqueness of his achievement.) His perspective, by professional standards, is inconsistent. It constantly adapts itself to the next sight in view; rather than being a standing static perspective, it is a walking one. (I think of the ghost of Tony Godwin who loved walking in Manhattan.) And the same creative inconsistency determines the eye-level. Things are seen either face to face as on the sidewalk, or from above, at about the height of a tenement roof. These are the two levels at which he must have observed most as a kid: playing on the tenement roof near the washing, or on the street at the foot of the fire-escapes. Which level he chooses depends upon what he is depicting: people — even if distant — are seen face to face; traffic is seen from above; apartment windows are seen as if you are level with them; Brooklyn Bridge is seen from below, but the river is seen from high above. Thus each painting offers, not an instant view, a postcard, but an amalgam of visual experience, a sequence of memories. Hence the likeness. Hence the face that those who have lived in these streets, *recognise* corner after corner although Fasanella has "invented" them.

A modern city, however, is not only a place, it is also in itself, long before it is painted, a series of images, a circuit of messages. A city teaches and conditions by its appearances, its facades and its plan. No city more dramatically than New York which served for at least fifty years (1870-1924) as a unique landing-stage and breaking-in ground for millions of immigrants who had come from distant villages or ghettoes or small towns.

The city demonstrated to the newly arrived what they had

97

to forget and what they had to learn. Nobody planned what New York taught. Its lessons were by example. In being what it was, it laid down its laws. At a profound level, Fasanella's paintings are about some of the lessons which the look of the city taught as law.

The most insistent feature of his paintings are windows. It is through its windows that the city speaks to him. Apartment windows, factory windows, shop-windows, office windows. In the tenements the windows are as repetitive as the bricks, although each is distinct. Sometimes a person is looking out. Yet the window-figures are different from those in the street. Each person in the street has her or his own silhouette and character. (He has a very sharp eye for character.) The window-figures are no more than signs within the rectangle of their window frame. In the great triptych of Manhattan the whole elevation of the city consists of framed windows, interspersed with publicity hoardings which resemble large windows.

Each window frames the locus of a private or social activity. Each frame contains the sign of a lived experience. The triptych as a whole assembles the sum of these signs of experience, which are massed together according to a visible law of accumulation, brick upon brick, storey upon storey, window by window. The city has grown like a honeycomb: unlike a honeycomb each cell, each window looks different. Yet these differences, which must express individual memories, hopes, choices, despair, cancel each other out and each set is always replaceable. (When the lodger dies or disappears, the room is re-let.) What continues day and night, year after year, is the frame of the city. The rest is like daily newsprint. This is the first lesson.

The windows disclose what is inside their buildings. Only *disclose* is the wrong word, for it suggests that before the disclosure, there was a secret. The windows *present* the life or lives of their building. They present their interiors in such a way as to show that they were never interiors. Nothing has an interior. Everything is exteriority. The whole city, in this sense, is like an eviscerated animal.

To emphasise this exteriority Fasanella often strips away part of a wall to show an entire living space as just another component of the elevation. And all these components (unlike the figures in the street or the traffic, who enjoy the freedom of a kind of space, even if it is finally illusory) are deliberately two-dimensional signs.

The typical surface of the new urbanism, not apparent in these paintings of New York which are twenty years old or more, but increasingly apparent in recently designed environments, is the shining surface of the mirror, of chrome, polished metal, polyesters, the surface which, by reflecting what is in front of it, denies what is behind it.

Fasanella often chalks on his sidewalks. Names. Dates. Insults. Sometimes single words: KISS, LOVE. What even such words evoke can only be rendered by a sign, like the lettering on the shop fronts to announce MEAT or LIQUOR, because the city has done away with all space for what lies behind or within. The only inner space sanctioned is that of the safe. This is the second lesson.

I am of course ignoring what Fasanella loved in Manhattan, because I am writing about the lessons of the place, and not about the people and the ingenuity with which they often resisted the lessons. Nevertheless a very intimate painting like *Family Supper* leads us to the same conclusion.

The family is Fasanella's. In the centre is his mother. On the right wall is one of his own paintings of his father, the iceman, crucified on a wall of bricks, his head clamped in the ice-tongs with which he worked. On the back wall is a second painting, this time of his mother with his sister and

99

himself standing on chairs in front of another wooden cross, against a brick wall between window frames. Every person and object in this kitchen is a memorial to what happened *within* his family. But the way it is painted — and here the truthfulness to experience of the "primitive" painting method reveals itself — *the way it is painted* makes everything in it continuous and entirely homogeneous with the exterior walls and elevation which surround it. The linoleum is painted like a street wall. The food on the dresser shelf like a shop window display. The bare electric light bulb like a street lamp. The electricity meter like a water hydrant. The backs of the chairs like railings.

Objectively space exists in Manhattan. It is a scarce and enormously valuable commodity. Sometimes Fasanella puts up a hoarding which ironically announces: SPACE TO LET. Yet this commodity, this space, is not *inhabitable,* except in purely physical terms. What has evacuated it? What makes the family kitchen no more than a cupboard off the street?

The answers are not only those which first spring to mind: overcrowding, poverty, insecurity. These phenomena existed in the countryside, yet a peasant house could still remain an enclosure, a refuge. What destroyed, invaded, the interior of the tenement home were even more basic economic processes. The home was not a store: on the contrary, the *store* was where you had to purchase each day the wherewithal to live. The wherewithal was paid for by so many hours of wage-labour. The time of the city — the time of wage hours — dominated every home. There was no refuge from this time. The home never contained the fruits of labour, a surplus, of either goods or time. Home is no more than a lodging house. This is the third lesson.

In the 1920's Brecht wrote a poem called *On The Crushing Impact of the Cities*. It ends like this:

> "So short was time
> That between morning and evening
> There was no noon
> And already on the old familiar ground
> Stood mountains of concrete."

Just as capital is compelled continually to reproduce itself, so its culture is one of unending anticipation. What-is-to-come, what-is-to-be-gained empties what-is. The immigrant proletariat, unable to return home, suffering from being who they were, yearned to become, or for their children to become, American. They saw no hope but to exchange themselves for the future. And although the desperation of this wager was specifically immigrant, the mechanism has become more and more typical of developed capitalism.

Time, they often say in New York, is money. This can also mean that money is what time is like. Money, being purely quantitative, has no content, but it can be exchanged for content: it purchases. The same has become true of time: it, too, is now being exchanged for the content it lacks. Work-time for wages, wages for the unlived time "encapsuled" in the purchase: the "speed" of the automobile, the eternal present of the television screen, the time "saved" in a hundred household appliances, the peace of the retirement pension to come, etc. etc. The fourth lesson of the city is pie in the sky, in which the denial of space and time combine.

Photographs of Manhattan, often make the island look like a monument. Fasanella's paintings show it as the most temporary and make-shift of stations. In truth, nothing can be kept there. This is why he inscribes in protest on the brick wall of a tenement building, a plea, which challenges all of

101

the city's lessons, as do his paintings: *Lest We Forget.*

This plea might be mistaken for nostalgia. It is not. It is a frontal protest against what the modern city, with its empty space and time, imposes: impersonal ahistoricity. It is on the site of such a protest that the only forces capable of defeating urban dehumanisation can meet and join forces.

1978

La Tour and Humanism

There is no doubt that Georges de La Tour existed. He was born in Lorraine in 1593 and he died in 1652. He probably painted most — or all — of the pictures that are now accredited to him, as well as others which have been destroyed. Yet the personality and oeuvre of La Tour are, in a sense, a modern creation.

After his death, his work and name was forgotten or ignored for nearly three centuries. In the 1920s and 1930s, one or two French art historians began to be interested in a few works then thought to be by him, an obscure provincial painter. Their interest may have been aroused because of a certain formal similarity between La Tour and the work of the post-Impressionists. In the winter of 1934, eleven of his paintings were included in an exhibition called *Painters of Reality* held at the Orangerie in Paris. They made an immediate and very great impact. After the war, art historians and curators all over the world began searching for new works and for information until, in 1972, they were able to present, at the same Orangerie, 31 pictures considered to be by the master himself and 20 copies or doubtful works.

The genius of La Tour has been reborn in the 20th century. What is the likely relation between the reborn genius and the original one? The question can never be completely answered, yet I am sceptical of the answers which have been assumed. La Tour was not quite what we are making him out to be.

The distortions are partly the result of recent French history. La Tour was rediscovered in the period of the Popular Front and his example was immediately put to use to further the idea of a popular democratic French tradition of culture. After the war, through a large New York exhibition, La Tour was presented to, and accepted by, the

103

outside world as a symbolic figure representing the victorious popular soul of France. Here is a typical quotation from a book written at the time in French:

"One might quote many illustrious names through the centuries. Three will suffice. Poussin, Watteau, Delacroix .

. . .but besides these great artists, for whom painting is a magic interpretation of the most profound thoughts and the most beautiful dreams, there is another kind of artist, apparently less elevated, but who brings no less honour to France. Indeed one of France's greatest claims is to have produced such artists, who do not exist elsewhere. These artists are profoundly modest. They choose to remain very close to nature, and with subjects which elsewhere are despised, or mocked, or made rhetorical, they say something very simple whose originality is scarcely at first discernible. Yet those who have eyes to see and a heart to feel, will come to recognise the nobility of their aspirations: their search for the truth without prejudice, without compromise, driven on by an emotion of sympathy which unites all men.''

And so it has continued. The frontispiece of the catalogue of the 1972 exhibition showed a single candle burning in front of a mirror. It burnt with holiness. Reproductions and Christmas cards of La Tour's work persuade the public of a consumer society that what they really aspire to is simplicity and humanist reverence.

Yet how does this accord with the facts of La Tour's life, or the real nature of his work? The facts are scanty but they are worth considering. La Tour was the son of a baker from a peasant family. He was able to marry — perhaps as a result of his evident promise as a painter — the daughter of a small local aristocrat. He went to live and work in her town, Lunéville, where he was highly successful as a painter, earned a lot of money and became one of the richest local landowners. During the thirty years' war which ravaged the countryside, he owed allegiance first to the Duke of Lorraine and later, after the French victory over the Duke, to the King of France. In the municipal records of the town there is a strong hint that he profiteered out of grain during the war famines. In 1646 the populace, in an appeal addressed to

105

their exiled Duke, complained against the arrogance, wealth and unjust privileges of the painter La Tour. Meanwhile the same populace were forced to pay for each of his major paintings, offered as gifts to the French Governor of Nancy. In 1648, a record shows that La Tour paid ten francs damages to a man whom he had beaten up in unknown circumstances. Two years later another record indicates that he had to pay 7.20 francs for the medical care of a peasant whom he had attacked when he found him trespassing on his land.

The bare outline of his life would suggest that La Tour was ambitious, hard-dealing, violent, fairly unscrupulous and successful. One must, however, beware of making unhistorical moral judgments. Many of the land-owning class in that part of France profiteered out of the thirty years' war. Nor is a great painter obliged to lead an exemplary moral life. Yet nevertheless between La Tour, the detested richest citizen of Lunéville, and La Tour, the painter of simple peasants, beggars, ascetic saints and Magdalenes renouncing the world, there is a certain contradiction.

Ever since his rebirth, La Tour has been labelled a *"Caravaggiste."* And it is true that his "popular" subject matter and his use of light suggest the indirect influence of Caravaggio. The spirit of the two painters' work, however, could scarcely be more opposed.

Here, in fact, the example of Caravaggio may illuminate a little the contradiction to which I referred above. Look at Caravaggio's *Death of the Virgin*. Caravaggio was involved in countless brawls and beatings-up. He even killed a man. He lived in the underworld of Rome. He painted those he lived beside. He painted them with his own emotions, he saw his own excesses in their very condition. That is to say: he is *in* the situation he paints. He lacked any sense of self-preservation, and this so coincided with those he painted —

106

and what he painted — that he lent his own life to his images. In such a context it is impossible to talk of conventional morality. We either walk past the *Death of the Virgin* or we mourn her. That is how little contradiction there is in Caravaggio. By contrast, La Tour is never *in* the situation he paints. He is distanced from it. The distance is the measure of his self-preservation. And within that space moral questions can legitimately arise.

La Tour's early paintings depict poor peasants (sometimes presented as saints), street musicians, beggars, card sharpers and fortune tellers. A painting of a seated old man, half-blind, mouth gaping, arthritic hands on the wooden hurdy-gurdy resting on his lap, is particularly striking. For three reasons: the pain of confrontation with such implied misery; the formal colour harmony of the painting; and the fact that the man's flesh is painted as though it were a substance no different in kind from the leather of his shoes, the stones at his feet or the cloth of his cloak. This "rejection" of the flesh is more explicit in two paintings of St Jerome, who kneels, nude, his skin like the paper of the bible open before him, a blood-stained scourge of rope in his hand with which he has been chastising himself. Is the detachment of such images holy, or merely unfeeling? Are they the result of confronting the suffering and despair to be seen on every side at that time in Lorraine, or did they serve to make the sight of such suffering easier to accept? The *sight,* not the *experience*, for, as I have emphasised these images are seen entirely from the exterior; they are like still-lifes.

The other early pictures of card-players and tricksters can perhaps answer this question. Once more the painting is clean and harmonious. Once again, flesh is painted as though it were an insensate material — wax or wood or pastry — the eyes like bits of fruit. But there is no suffering now. There are simply two games being played. The game of cards (or the game of palm-reading) and, under cover of this, the game of cheating or robbing the rich young man who is fair game. The paintings reveal no psychological insight. The interest of these paintings is schematic — in every sense of that word. There is the formal scheme of the painting. The scheme of the game — its rules, its symbolic language; and finally the scheme of the cheating of the young man, its planning, its sign-language of gestures and looks, its ineluctability.

La Tour, I believe, saw the whole of life as a scheme over which nobody on earth had any control, a scheme revealed in prophecy and the scriptures. Accordingly, the existence of beggars becomes no more than a sign, St. Jerome no more than a moral injunction; people are transformed into ciphers. Yet the total faith of the middle ages has gone. Scientific observation has begun. The individuality of the thinker and artist cannot be brushed aside or undone. Consequently the painter cannot simply submit to a God-given iconography. He must invent. Yet if he accepts such a view of the world (the world as unquestionable scheme) the only way he can invent is by imitating God, modestly and piously, within the small domain of his own art. Accepting the world as scheme, he makes his own harmonious visual schemes out of it. Before the world he is helpless *except as a maker of pictures*. The abstract formality of La Tour was consolation for a moral defeat.

La Tour's later works seem to bear out this interpretation. In 1636 the French governor set fire to the town of Lunéville rather than let it fall into the hands of the Duke's troops. The town blazed all night. An eye-witness testified that you could read in the streets by the light of the flames. A month later the French captured the town and sacked it. These incidents were a turning point in La Tour's life. Many of his paintings must have been destroyed, likewise some of his property. When he re-established himself in the town, be began to produce his night pieces, his candlelight pictures, for which, then as now, he became best known.

Most of these night scenes imply a different level — but not a different type — of religious preoccupation. The candlelight disembodies and derationalises. And the frontier between being and non-being, appearance and illusion, consciousness and dream, becomes vague. When there is more than one figure, it is hard to be sure whether each is real or only the dream projection of the other. Every lit form proposes the possibility that it is no more than an apparition. Did I see it? Or did I dream it? If I shut my eyes, it is dark again. La Tour is exorcising his doubts. (Is it not just possible that the painting of St Peter weeping is a self-portrait?) They are pictures like monologues or prayers. They do not discourse with the world directly. And so the problem of the painted person, seen as a mere cipher in God's scheme or the painter's, is removed — because what we are presented with is no longer the world, but the night of the artist's soul.

Within these limits, three of the night paintings are masterpieces. The Magdalene with a mirror. Here everything has been eliminated except what the scheme of the painting and the scheme of the message (scripture) requires. We see her head in profile. Her near hand touches the skull on the table before her. Both hand and skull are silhouetted dark, dead, against the light. Her far arm is lit and living. Thus she is divided into two. She looks into a mirror. What we see in the mirror is the skull. The balance is mathematical and dreamlike.

The second is of St Joseph as a carpenter. He bends forward, working. The candlelight burnishes his flesh which is as opaque as wood. The child Jesus holds up the candle.

His childish hand, which shields it, is made transparent by the light, and his lit face is like a window at night seen from the outside. Again, the formal painting and the message (the contrast between childhood and age; the opaque and the transparent, experience and innocence) are entirely uninterrupted and perfectly balanced.

The third masterpiece is one I cannot explain. It is the so-called *Woman With A Flea*. She sits half-naked in the candlelight. Her hands are pressed against each other beneath her breasts. Some say that she is squashing a flea between her thumbnails. I read her hands placed there as a gesture of conviction. The spirit of the painting is unlike any other by La Tour which has survived. It almost confirms the usual view of his art. The woman sitting there is neither symbol nor cipher. The candlelight is gentle; there are no apparitions. She is there. The climate of her body fills the picture. Perhaps La Tour was in love with her.

To appreciate these three works is not, however, to encounter "an emotion of sympathy uniting all men." The formal aesthetic perfection to which La Tour aspired was his special solution to a religious and social problem about, precisely, the *meaning* of other men: a problem which, in its own terms, he found insoluble.

1972

Francis Bacon and
Walt Disney

A blood-stained figure on a bed. A carcase with splints on it. A man on a chair smoking. One walks past his paintings as if through some gigantic institution. A man on a chair turning. A man holding a razor. A man shitting.

What is the meaning of the events we see? The painted figures are all quite indifferent to one another's presence or plight. Are we, as we walk past them, the same? A photograph of Bacon with his sleeves rolled up shows that his forearms closely resemble those of many of the men he paints. A woman crawls along a rail like a child. In 1971, according to the magazine *Connaissance des Arts,* Bacon became the first of the top ten most important living artists. A man sits naked with torn newspaper around his feet. A man stares at a blind cord. A man reclines in a vest on a stained red couch. There are many faces which move, and as they move they give an impression of pain. There has never been painting quite like this. It relates to the world we live in. But how?

To begin with a few facts:

1. Francis Bacon is the only British painter this century to have gained an international influence.

2. His work is remarkably consistent, from the first paintings to the most recent. One is confronted by a fully articulated world-view.

3. Bacon is a painter of extraordinary skill, a master. Nobody who is familiar with the problems of figurative oil-painting can remain unimpressed by his solutions. Such mastery, which is rare, is the result of great dedication and extreme lucidity about the medium.

4. Bacon's work has been unusually well written about. Writers such as David Sylvester, Michel Leiris and Lawrence Gowing have discussed its internal implications

111

with great eloquence. By "internal" I mean the implications of its own propositions within its own terms.

Bacon's work is centred on the human body. The body is usually distorted, whereas what clothes or surrounds it is relatively undistorted. Compare the raincoat with the torso, the umbrella with the arm, the cigarette stub with the mouth. According to Bacon himself, the distortions undergone by face or body are the consequence of his searching for a way of making the paint "come across directly on to the nervous system." Again and again, he refers to the nervous system of painter and spectator. The nervous system for him is independent of the brain. The kind of figurative painting which appeals to the brain, he finds illustrational and boring.

"I've always hoped to put over things as directly and rawly as I possibly can, and perhaps if a thing comes across directly, they feel that it is horrific."

To arrive at this rawness which speaks directly to the nervous system, Bacon relies heavily on what he calls "the accident." "In my case, I feel that anything I've ever liked at all has been the result of an accident on which I've been able to work."

The "accident" occurs in his painting when he makes "involuntary marks" upon the canvas. His "instinct" then finds in these marks a way of developing the image. A developed image is one that is both factual and suggestive to the nervous system.

"Isn't it that one wants a thing to be as factual as possible, and yet at the same time as deeply suggestive or deeply unlocking of areas of sensation other than simple illustrating of the object that you set out to do? Isn't that what art is all about?"

For Bacon the "unlocking" object is always the human body. Other things in his painting (chairs, shoes, blinds,

112

lamp switches, newspapers) are merely illustrated.

"What I want to do is to distort the thing far beyond appearance, but in the distortion to bring it back to a recording of the appearance."

Interpreted as process, we now see that this means the following. The appearance of a body suffers the accident of involuntary marks being made upon it. Its distorted image then comes across directly on to the nervous system of the viewer (or painter), who rediscovers the appearance of the body through or beneath the marks it bears.

Apart from the inflicted marks of the painting-accident, there are also sometimes *painted marks* on a body or on a mattress. These are, more or less obviously, traces of body fluids — blood, semen, perhaps shit. When they occur, the stains on the canvas are like stains on a surface which has actually touched the body.

The double-meaning of the words which Bacon has always used when talking about his painting (*accident, rawness, marks*), and perhaps even the double-meaning of his own name, seem to be part of the vocabulary of an obsession, an experience which probably dates back to the beginning of his self-consciousness. There are no alternatives offered in Bacon's world, no ways out. Consciousness of time or change does not exist. Bacon often starts working on a painting from an image taken from a photograph. A photograph records for a moment. In the process of painting, Bacon seeks the accident which will turn that moment into all moments. In life, the moment which ousts all preceding and following moments is most commonly a moment of physical pain. And pain may be the ideal to which Bacon's obsession aspires. Nevertheless, the content of his paintings, the content which constitutes their appeal, has little to do with pain. As often, the obsession is a distraction and the real content lies elsewhere.

Bacon's work is said to be an expression of the anguished loneliness of western man. His figures are isolated in glass cases, in arenas of pure colour, in anonymous rooms, or even just within themselves. Their isolation does not preclude their being watched. (The triptych form, in which each figure is isolated within his own canvas and yet is visible to the others, is symptomatic.) His figures are alone, but they are utterly without privacy. The marks they bear, their wounds, look self-inflicted. But self-inflicted in a highly special sense. Not by an individual but by the species, Man — because, under conditions of such universal solitude, the distinction between individual and species becomes meaningless.

Bacon is the opposite of an apocalyptic painter who envisages the worst is likely. For Bacon, the worst has already happened. The worst that has happened has nothing to do with the blood, the stains, the viscera. The worst is that man has come to be seen as mindless.

The worst had already happened in the *Crucifixion* of 1944. The bandages and the screams are already in place — as also is the aspiration towards ideal pain. But the necks end in mouths. The top half of the face does not exist. The skull is missing.

Later, the worst is evoked more subtly. The anatomy is left intact, and man's inability to reflect is suggested by what happens around him and by his expression — or lack of it. The glass cases, which contain friends or a Pope, are reminiscent of those in which animal behaviour-patterns can be studied. The props, the trapeze chairs, the railings, the cords, are like those with which cages are fitted. Man is an unhappy ape. But if he knows it, he isn't. And so it is necessary to show that man cannot know. Man is an unhappy ape without knowing it. It is not a brain but a perception which separates the two species. This is the

114

axiom on which Bacon's art is based.

During the early 1950s, Bacon appeared to be interested in facial expressions. But not, as he admits, for what they expressed.

"In fact, I wanted to paint the scream more than the horror. And I think if I had really thought about what causes somebody to scream — the horror that produces a scream — it would have made the screams that I tried to paint more successful. In fact, they were too abstract. They originally started through my always having been very moved by movements of the mouth and the shape of the mouth and the teeth. I like, you may say, the glitter and colour that comes from the mouth, and I've always hoped in a sense to be able to paint the mouth like Monet painted a sunset."

In the portraits of friends like Isabel Rawsthorne, or in some of the new self-portraits, one is confronted with the expression of an eye, sometimes two eyes. But study these expressions; read them. Not one is self-reflective. The eyes look out from their condition, dumbly, on to what surrounds them. They do not know what has happened to them; and their poignancy lies in their ignorance. Yet what has happened to them? The rest of their faces have been contorted with expressions which are not their own — which, indeed, are not expressions at all (because there is nothing behind them to be expressed), but are events created by accident in collusion with the painter.

Not altogether by accident, however. Likeness remains — and in this Bacon uses all his mastery. Normally, likeness defines character, and character in man is inseparable from mind. Hence the reason why some of these portraits, unprecedented in the history of art, although never tragic, are very haunting, We see character as the empty cast of a consciousness that is absent. Once again, the worst has happened. Living man has become his own mindless spectre.

In the larger figure-compositions, where there is more than one personage, the lack of expression is matched by the total unreceptivity of the other figures. They are all proving to each other, all the time, that they can have no expression. Only grimaces remain.

Bacon's view of the absurd has nothing in common with existentialism, or with the work of an artist like Samuel Beckett. Beckett approaches despair as a result of questioning, as a result of trying to unravel the language of the conventionally given answers. Bacon questions nothing, unravels nothing. He accepts the worst has happened.

 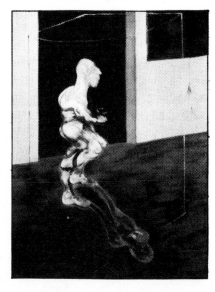

His lack of alternatives, within his view of the human condition, is reflected in the lack of any thematic development in his life's work. His progress, during 30 years, is a technical one of getting the worst into sharper focus. He succeeds, but at the same time the reiteration makes the worst less credible. That is his paradox. As you walk through room after room it becomes clear that you can live with the worst, that you can go on painting it again and again, that you can turn it into more and more elegant art, that you can put velvet and gold frames round it, that other people will buy it to hang on the walls of the rooms where they eat. It begins to seem that Bacon may be a charlatan. Yet he is not. And his fidelity to his own obsession ensures that the paradox of his art yields a consistent truth, though it may not be the truth he intends.

Bacon's art is, in effect, conformist. It is not with Goya or the early Eisenstein that he should be compared, but with Walt Disney. Both men make propositions about the alienated behaviour of our societies; and both, in a different way, persuade the viewer to accept what is. Disney makes alienated behaviour look funny and sentimental and, therefore, acceptable. Bacon interprets such behaviour in terms of the worst possible having already happened, and so proposes that both refusal and hope are pointless. The surprising formal similarities of their work — the way limbs are distorted, the overall shapes of bodies, the relation of figures to background and to one another, the use of neat tailor's clothes, the gesture of hands, the range of colours used — are the result of both men having complementary attitudes to the same crisis.

Disney's world is also charged with vain violence. The ultimate catastrophe is always in the offing. His creatures have both personality and nervous reactions; what they lack (almost) is mind. If, before a cartoon sequence by Disney, one read and believed the caption, *There is nothing else,* the film would strike us as horrifically as a painting by Bacon.

Bacon's paintings do not comment, as is often said, on any actual experience of loneliness, anguish or metaphysical doubt; nor do they comment on social relations, bureaucracy, industrial society or the history of the 20th century. To do any of these things they would have to be concerned with consciousness. What they do is to demonstrate how alienation may provoke a longing for its own absolute form — which is mindlessness. This is the consistent truth demonstrated, rather than expressed, in Bacon's work.

1972

An Article of Faith

The de Stijl movement, which was centred upon a small magazine of the same name, was founded in Holland in 1917 by the critic and painter Theo van Doesburg. The movement ceased when he died in 1931. It was always a small and fairly informal movement. Members left and others joined. Its first years were probably its most originally productive ones. Members then included the painters Mondriaan and Bart van der Leck, the designer Gerrit Rietveld and the architect J. J. P. Oud. Both the magazine and its artists were, during the whole de Stijl period, relatively obscure and unrecognised.

The magazine was called *The Style* (de Stijl) because it was intended to demonstrate a modern style applicable to all problems of two and three dimensional design. Its articles and illustrations were seen as definitions, prototypes and blueprints for what could become man's total urban environment. The group was as opposed to hierarchic distinctions between different disciplines (painting, designing, town planning and so on) as it was to any cultivated individualism in any art.

The individual must lose and re-find himself in the universal. Art, they believed, had become the preliminary model by means of which man could discover how to control and order his whole environment. When that control was established, art might even disappear. Their vision was consciously social, iconoclastic and aesthetically revolutionary.

The fundamental elements of *The Style* style were the straight line, the right angle, the cross, the point, rectangular planes, an always convertible plastic space (quite distinct from the natural space of appearances), the three primary colours red, blue and yellow, a white ground and black lines. With these pure and rigorously abstract elements the de Stijl artists strove to represent and construct essential harmony.

The nature of this harmony was understood somewhat differently by different members of the group: for Mondriaan it was a quasi-mystical universal absolute: for Rietveld or the architect and civil engineer Van Eesteren it was the formal balance and the implied social meaning which they hoped to achieve in a particular work.

Let us consider a typical work, often referred to in the history books. The Red-Blue Chair (a wooden chair with arm-rests) designed by Rietveld.

The chair is made out of only two wooden elements: the board used for back and seat, and the square sections used for legs, frame and arms. There are no joints in the joiner's sense of the term. Wherever two or more sections meet, they are laid one on top of the other and each protrudes beyond the cross-over. The way in which the elements are painted — blue, red or yellow — emphasises the lightness and the intentional *obviousness* of the assembly.

You have the sense that the parts could be quickly re-assembled to make a small table, a bookcase or the model of a city. You are reminded of how children sometimes use coloured bricks for building an entire world. Yet there is little that is childish about this chair. Its mathematical proportions are exactly calculated and its implications attack in a logical manner a whole series of established attitudes and preoccupations.

This chair eloquently opposes values that still persist: the aesthetic of the hand-made, the notion that ownership bestows power and weight, the virtues of permanence and indestructibility, the love of mystery and secrets, the fear that technology threatens culture, the horror of the anonymous, the mystique and the rights of privilege. It

120

opposes all this in the name of its aesthetic, whilst remaining a (not very comfortable) armchair.

It proposes that for man to situate himself in the universe, he no longer requires God, or the example of nature, or rituals of class or state, or love of country: he requires precise vertical and horizontal coordinates. In these alone will he find the essential truth. And this truth will be inseparable from the style in which he lives. "The aim of nature is man," wrote Van Doesburg, "the aim of man is style."

The chair, hand-made, stands there like a chair waiting to be mass-produced: yet in certain ways it is as haunting as a painting by Van Gogh.

Why should such an austere piece of furniture have acquired — at least temporarily for us — a kind of poignancy?

An era ended in the early 1960s. During that era the idea of a different, transformed future remained a European and North American prerogative. Even when the future was considered negatively (*Brave New World, 1984*) it was conceived of in European terms.

Today, although Europe (east and west) and North America retain the technological means capable of transforming the world, they appear to have lost the political and spiritual initiative for bringing about any transformation. Thus today we can see the prophecies of the early European artistic avant-gardes in a different light. The continuity between us and them — such as we might have believed in an attenuated form only ten years ago — has now been broken. They are not for us to defend or attack. They are for us to examine so that we may begin to understand the other world-revolutionary possibilities which they and we failed to foresee or reckon with.

Up to 1914, during the first decade of this century, it was clear to all those who were compelled either by necessity or imagination to consider the forces of change at work, that the world was entering a period of uniquely fast transition. In the arts this atmosphere of promise and prophecy found its purest expression in cubism. Kahnweiler, dealer and friend of the cubists, wrote:

"I lived those seven years from 1907 to 1914 with my painter friends . . . what occurred at that time in the plastic arts will be understood only if one bears in mind that a new epoch was being born, in which man (all mankind in fact) was undergoing a transformation more radical than any other known within historical times."

On the political left, the same conviction of promise was expressed in a fundamental belief in internationalism.

There are rare historical moments of convergence when

developments in numerous fields enter a period of similar qualitative change before diverging into a multiplicity of new terms. Few of those who live through such a moment can grasp the full significance of what is happening. But all are aware of change: the future, instead of offering continuity, appears to advance towards them.

The ten years before 1914 constituted such a moment. When Apollinaire wrote:

I am everywhere or rather I start to be everywhere
It is I who am starting this thing of the centuries to come,

he was not indulging in idle fancy but responding intuitively to the potential of a concrete situation.

Yet nobody at that time, not even Lenin, foresaw how prolonged, confused and terrible the process of transformation was going to be. Above all, nobody realised how far-reaching would be the effects of the coming *inversion* of politics — that is to say the increasing predominance of ideology over politics. It was a time which offered more long-term and perhaps more accurate perspectives than we can hope for today: but, in the light of later events, we can also see it as a time of relative political innocence, albeit justified.

Soon such innocence ceased to be justified. Too much evidence had to be denied to maintain it: notably the conduct of the First World War (not its mere outbreak) and the widespread popular acquiescence in it. The October revolution may at first have seemed to confirm earlier forms of political innocence but the failure of the revolution to spread throughout the rest of Europe and all the consequences of that failure within the Soviet Union itself should then have put a final end to them. What in fact happened is that most people remained politically innocent at the price of denying experience — and this in itself contributed further to the political-ideological inversion.

123

By 1917 Mondriaan was claiming that de Stijl was the result of pursuing the logic of cubism further than the cubists had dared to do. To some degree this was true. The de Stijl artists purified cubism and extracted a system from it. (It was by means of this system that cubism began to influence architecture.) But this purification took place at a time when reality was revealing itself as more tragic and far less pure than the cubists of 1911 could ever have imagined.

Dutch neutrality in the war and a national tendency to revert to a belief in Calvinist absolutes obviously played a part in influencing de Stijl theories. But this is not the point I wish to make. (To understand the relation between de Stijl and its Dutch background, one should consult H. L. C. Jaffé's pioneering work, *De Stijl 1917-31*.) The important point is that what were still intuitively real prophecies for the cubists became utopian dreams for the artists of de Stijl.

De Stijl utopianism was compounded of a subjective retreat away from reality in the name of invisible universal principles — and the dogmatic assertion that objectivity was all that mattered. The two opposing but interdependent tendencies are illustrated by the following two statements:

"The painters of this group, wrongly called 'abstractionists,' do not have a preference for a certain subject, knowing well enough that the painter has his subject within himself: plastic relations. For the true painter, the painter of relations, this fact contains his entire conception of the world." (Van Doesburg)

"We come to see that the principal problem in plastic art is not to avoid representation of objects, but to be as objective as possible." (Mondriaan)

A similar contradiction can now be seen in the aesthetic of the movement. This was confidently based upon values born

124

of the machine and modern technology: values of order, precision and mathematics. Yet the programme of this aesthetic was formulated when a chaotic, untidy, unpredictable and desperate ideological factor was becoming the crucial one in social development.

Let me be quite clear. I am not suggesting that the de Stijl programme should have been more directly political. Indeed the political programmes of the left were soon to suffer from an exactly equivalent contradiction. A subjective retreat from reality leading to the dogmatic stressing of the need for pure objectivity was of the essence of Stalinism. Nor do I wish to suggest that de Stijl artists were personally insincere. I wish to treat them — as they would surely have wished — as a significant part of history. It goes without saying that we can sympathise with the aims of de Stijl. Yet what, for us, now seems missing from de Stijl?

What is missing is an awareness of the importance of subjective experience as a historical factor. Instead, subjectivity is simultaneously indulged in and denied. The equivalent social and political mistake was to trust in economic determinism. It was a mistake which dominated the whole era that has just ended.

Artists, however, reveal more about themselves than most politicians: and often know more about themselves. This is why their testimony is historically so valuable.

The strain of denying subjectivity whilst indulging in it is poignantly evident in the following manifesto of Van Doesburg's:

"White! There is the spiritual colour of our times, the clear-cut attitude that directs all our actions. Not gray, not ivory white, but pure white. White! There's the colour of the new age, the colour which signifies the whole epóch: ours, that of the perfectionist, of purity and of certainty. White, just that.

125

Behind us the 'brown' of decay and of academism, the 'blue' of divisionism, the cult of the blue sky, of gods with greenish whiskers and of the spectre. White, pure white.''

Is it only imagination that makes us feel now a similar almost unconscious doubt expressed in the Rietveld chair? That chair haunts us not as a chair but as an article of faith . . .

1968

Between Two Colmars

I first went to Colmar to look at the Grünewald Altarpiece in the winter of 1963. I went a second time ten years later. I didn't plan it that way. During the intervening years a great deal had changed. Not at Colmar, but, generally, in the world, and also in my life. The dramatic point of change was exactly half-way through that decade. In 1968, hopes, nurtured more or less underground for years, were born in several places in the world and given their names: and in the same year, these hopes were categorically defeated. This became clearer in retrospect. At the time many of us tried to shield ourselves from the harshness of the truth. For instance, at the beginning of 1969, we still thought in terms of a second 1968 possibly recurring.

This is not the place for an analysis of what changed in the alignment of political forces on a world scale. Enough to say that the road was cleared for what, later, would be called *normalization*. Many thousands of lives were changed too. But this will not be read in the history books. (There was a comparable, although very different, watershed in 1848, and its effects on the life of a generation are recorded, not in the histories, but in Flaubert's *Sentimental Education*.) When I look around at my friends — and particularly those who were (or still are) politically conscious — I see how the long-term direction of their lives was altered or deflected at that moment just as it might have been by a private event: the onset of an illness, an unexpected recovery, a bankruptcy. I imagine that if they looked at me, they would see something similar.

Normalization means that between the different political systems, which share the control of almost the entire world, anything can be exchanged under the single condition that nothing anywhere is radically changed. The present is

127

assumed to be continuous, the continuity allowing for technological development.

A time of expectant hopes (as before 1968) encourages one to think of oneself as unflinching. Everything needs to be faced. The only danger seems to be evasion or sentimentality. Harsh truth will aid liberation. This principle becomes so integral to one's thinking that it is accepted without question. One is aware of how it might be otherwise. Hope is a marvellous focusing lens. One's eye becomes fixed to it. And one can examine anything.

The altarpiece, no less than a Greek tragedy or 19th century novel, was originally planned to encompass the totality of a life and an explanation of the world. It was painted on hinged panels of wood. When these were shut, those before the altar saw the Crucifixion, flanked by St. Anthony and St. Sebastian. When the panels were opened, they saw a Concert of Angels and a Madonna and Child, flanked by an Annunciation and Resurrection. When the panels were opened once again, they saw the apostles and some church dignitaries flanked by paintings about the life of St. Anthony. The altarpiece was commissioned for a hospice at Isenheim by the Antonite order. The hospice was for victims of the plague and syphilis. The altarpiece was used to help victims come to terms with their suffering.

On my first visit to Colmar I saw the Crucifixion as the key to the whole altarpiece and I saw disease as the key to the Crucifixion. "The longer I look, the more convinced I become that for Grünewald disease represents the actual state of man. Disease is not for him the prelude to death — as modern man tends to fear; it is the condition of life." This is what I wrote in 1963. I ignored the hinging of the Altarpiece. With my lens of hope, I had no need of the painted panels of hope. I saw Christ in the Resurrection "as pallid with the pallor of death"; I saw the Virgin in the

Annunciation responding to the Angel as if "to the news of an incurable disease"; in the Madonna and Child I seized upon the fact that the swaddling cloth was the tattered (infected) rag which would later serve as loin cloth in the Crucifixion.

This view of the work was not altogether arbitrary. The beginning of the 16th century was felt and experienced in many parts of Europe as a time of damnation. And undoubtedly this experience *is* in the Altarpiece. Yet not exclusively so. But in 1963 I saw only this, only the bleakness. I had no need of anything else.

Ten years later, the gigantic crucified body still dwarfed the mourners in the painting and the onlooker outside it. This time I thought: the European tradition is full of images of torture and pain, most of them sadistic. How is it that this, which is one of the harshest and most pain-filled of all, is an exception? How is it painted?

It is painted inch by inch. No contour, no cavity, no rise within the contours, reveals a moment's flickering of the intensity of depiction. Depiction is pinned to the pain suffered. Since no part of the body escapes pain, the depiction can nowhere slack its precision. The cause of the pain is irrelevant; all that matters now is the faithfulness of the depiction. This faithfulness came from the empathy of love.

Love bestows innocence. It has nothing to forgive. The person loved is not the same as the person seen crossing the street or washing her face. Nor exactly the same as the person living his (or her) own life and experience, for he (or she) cannot remain innocent.

Who then is the person loved? A mystery, whose identity is confirmed by nobody except the lover. How well Dostoevsky saw this. Love is solitary even though it joins.

The person loved is the being who continues when the person's own actions and egocentricity have been dissolved. Love recognises a person before the act and the *same* person after it. It invests this person with a value which is untranslatable into virtue.

Such love might be epitomised by the love of a mother for her child. Passion is only one mode of love. Yet there are differences. A child is in process of becoming. A child is incomplete. In what he is, at any given moment, he may be remarkably complete. In the passage between moments, however, he becomes dependent, and his incompleteness becomes obvious. The love of the mother connives with the child. She imagines him more complete. Their wishes become mixed, or they alternate. Like legs walking.

The discovery of a loved person, already formed and completed, is the onset of a passion.

One recognises those whom one does not love by their attainments. The attainments one finds important may differ from those which society in general acclaims. Nevertheless we take account of those we do not love according to the way they fill a contour, and to describe this contour we use comparative adjectives. Their overall "shape" is the sum of their attainments, as described by adjectives.

A person loved is seen in the opposite way. Their contour or shape is not a surface encountered but an horizon which borders. A person loved is recognised not by attainments but by the *verbs* which can satisfy that person. His or her needs may be quite distinct from those of the lover, but they create value: the value of that love.

For Grünewald the verb was *to paint.* To paint the life of Christ.

Empathy, carried to the degree which Grünewald carried it, may reveal an area of truth between the objective and subjective. Doctors and scientists working today on the phenomenology of pain might well study this painting. The distortions of form and proportion — the enlargement of the feet, the barrel-chesting of the torso, the elongation of the arms, the planting out of the fingers — may describe exactly the *felt* anatomy of pain.

I do not want to suggest that I saw more in 1973 than in 1963. I saw differently. That is all. The ten years do not necessarily mark a progress; in many ways they represent defeat.

The altarpiece is housed in a tall gallery with gothic windows near a river by some warehouses. During my second visit I was making notes and occasionally looking up at the Angel's Concert. The gallery was deserted except for the single guardian, an old man rubbing his hands in woollen gloves over a portable oil stove. I looked up and was aware that something had moved or changed. Yet I had heard nothing and the gallery was absolutely silent. Then I saw what had changed. The sun was out. Low in the winter sky, it shone directly through the gothic windows so that on the white wall opposite, their pointed arches were printed, with sharp edges, in light. I looked from the "window lights" on the wall to the light in the painted panels — the painted window at the far end of the painted chapel where the Annunciation takes place, the light that pours down the mountainside behind the Madonna, the great circle of light like an aurora borealis round the resurrected Christ. In each case the painted light held its own. It remained light; it did not disintegrate into coloured paint. The sun went in and the white wall lost its animation. The paintings retained their radiance.

The whole altarpiece, I now realised, is about darkness and light. The immense space of sky and plain behind the crucifixion — the plain of Alsace crossed by thousands of refugees fleeing war and famine — is deserted and filled with a darkness that appears final. In 1963 the light in the other panels seemed to me frail and artificial. Or, more accurately, frail and unearthly. (A light dreamt of in the darkness.) In 1973 I thought I saw that the light in these panels accords with the essential experience of light.

Only in rare circumstances is light uniform and constant. (Sometimes at sea; sometimes around high mountains.) Normally light is variegated or shifting. Shadows cross it. Some surfaces reflect more light than others. Light is not, as the moralists would have us believe, the constant polar opposite to darkness. Light flares out of darkness.

Look at the panels of the Madonna and the Angel's Consort. When it is not absolutely regular, light overturns the regular measurement of space. Light re-forms space as we perceive it. At first what is in light has a tendency to look nearer than what is in shadow. The village lights at night appear to bring the village closer. When one examines this phenomenon more closely, it becomes more subtle. Each concentration of light acts as a centre of imaginative attraction, so that in imagination one measures *from* it across the areas in shadow or darkness. And so there are as many articulated spaces as there are concentrations of light. Where one is actually situated establishes the primary space of a ground plan. But far from there a dialogue begins with each place in light, however distant, and each proposes another space and a different spatial articulation. Each place where there is brilliant light, prompts one to imagine oneself there. It is as though the seeing eye sees echoes of itself wherever the light is concentrated. This multiplicity is a kind of joy.

The attraction of the eye to light, the attraction of the organism to light as a source of energy, is basic. The attraction of the imagination to light is more complex because it involves the mind as a whole and therefore it involves comparative experience. We respond to physical modifications of light with distinct but infinitesimal modifications of spirit, high and low, hopeful and fearful. In front of most scenes one's experience of their light is divided in spatial zones of sureness and doubt. Vision advances from light to light like a figure walking on stepping stones.

Put these two observations, made above, together: hope attracts, radiates as a point, to which one wants to be near, from which one wants to measure. Doubt has no centre and is ubiquitous.

Hence the strength and fragility of Grünewald's light.

On the occasion of both my visits to Colmar it was winter, and the town was under the grip of a similar cold, the cold which comes off the plain and carries with it a reminder of hunger. In the same town, under similar physical conditions, I saw differently. It is a commonplace that the significance of a work of art changes as it survives. Usually however, this knowledge is used to distinguish between "them" (in the past) and "us" (now). There is a tendency to picture *them* and their reactions to art as being embedded in history, and at the same time to credit *ourselves* with an over-view, looking across from what we treat as the summit of history. The surviving work of art then seems to confirm our superior position. The aim of its survival was us.

This is illusion. There is no exemption from history. The first time I saw the Grünewald I was anxious to place *it* historically. In terms of medieval religion, the plague, medicine, the Lazar house. Now I have been forced to place myself historically.

In a period of revolutionary expectation, I saw a work of art which had survived as evidence of the past's despair; in a period which has to be endured, I see the same work miraculously offering a narrow pass across despair.

1973

Courbet and the Jura

No artist's work is reducible to *the* independent truth; like the artist's life — or yours or mine — the life's work constitutes its own valid or worthless truth. Explanations, analyses, interpretation, are no more than frames or lenses to help the spectator focus his attention more sharply on the work. The only justification for criticism is that it allows us to see more clearly.

Several years ago I wrote that two things needed explaining about Courbet because they remained obscure. First, the true nature of the materiality, the density, the weight of his images. Second, the profound reasons why his work so outraged the bourgeois world of art. The second question has since been brilliantly answered — not, surprisingly, by a French scholar — but by British and American ones: Timothy Clark in his two books, *Image of the People* and *The Absolute Bourgeois,* and Linda Nochlin in her book on *Realism.*

The first question, however, remains unanswered. The theory and programme of Courbet's realism have been socially and historically explained, but how did he practise it with his eyes and hands? What is the meaning of the unique way in which he rendered appearances? When he said: art is "the most complete expression of an existing thing," what did he understand by *expression?*

The region in which a painter passes his childhood and adolescence often plays an important part in the constitution of his vision. The Thames developed Turner. The cliffs around Le Havre were formative in the case of Monet. Courbet grew up in — and throughout his life painted and often returned to — the valley of the Loue on the western side of the Jura mountains. To consider the character of the countryside surrounding Ornans, his birthplace is, I believe, one way of constructing a frame which may bring his work into focus.

The region has an exceptionally high rainfall: approximately 51 inches a year, whereas the average on the French plains varies from 31 inches in the west to 16 inches in the centre. Most of this rain sinks through the limestone to form subterranean channels. The Loue, at its source, gushes out of the rocks as an already substantial river. It is a typical *karst* region, characterised by outcrops of limestone, deep valleys, caves and folds. On the horizontal strata of limestone there are often marl deposits which allow grass or trees to grow on top of the rock. One sees this formation — a very green landscape, divided near the sky by a horizontal bar of grey rock — in many of Courbet's paintings, including *The Burial at Ornans*. Yet I believe that the influence of this landscape and geology on Courbet was more than scenic.

Let us first try to visualise the mode of appearances in such a landscape in order to discover the perceptual habits it might encourage. Due to its folds, the landscape is *tall*: the sky is a long way off. The predominant colour is green: against this green the principal events are the rocks. The background to appearances in the valley is dark — as if something of the darkness of the caves and subterranean water has seeped into what is visible.

From this darkness whatever catches the light (the side of a rock, running water, the bough of a tree) emerges with a vivid, gratuitous but only partial (because much remains in shadow) clarity. It is a place where the visible is discontinuous. Or, to put it another way, where the visible cannot always be assumed and has to be grasped when it does make its appearance. Not only the abundant game, but the place's mode of appearances, created by its dense forests, steep slopes, waterfalls, twisting river — encourages one to develop the eyes of a hunter.

Many of these features are transposed into Courbet's art, even when the subjects are no longer his home landscape. An unusual number of his outdoor figure paintings have little or no sky in them (*The stonebreakers, Proudhon and his family, Girls on the banks of the Seine, The hammock,* most of the paintings of *Bathers*). The light is the lateral light of a forest, not unlike light underwater which plays tricks with perspective. What is disconcerting about the huge painting of the *Studio* is that the light of the painted wooded landscape on the easel is the light that suffuses the crowded Paris room. An exception to this general rule is the painting of *Bonjour Monsieur Courbet,* in which he depicts himself and his patron against the sky. This, however, was a painting consciously situated on the faraway plain of Montpelier.

I would guess that water occurs, in some form or another, in about two thirds of Courbet's paintings — often in the foreground. (The rural bourgeois house in which he was born juts out over the river. Running water must have been one of the first sights and sounds which he experienced). When water is absent from his paintings, the foreground forms are frequently reminiscent of the currents and swirls of running water (for example, *The woman with a parrot, The sleeping spinning girl*). The lacquered vividness of objects, which catch the light in his paintings, often recalls the brilliance of pebbles or fishes seen through water. The tonality of his painting of a trout underwater is the same as the tonality of his other paintings. There are whole landscapes by Courbet which might be landscapes reflected in a pond, their colour glistening on the surface, defying atmospheric perspective (for example, *The rocks at Mouthier*).

He usually painted on a dark ground, on which he painted darker still. The depth of his paintings is always due to darkness — even if, far above, there is an intensely blue sky;

in this his paintings are like wells. Wherever forms emerge
from the darkness into the light, he defines them by applying
a lighter colour, usually with a palette knife. Leaving aside
for the moment the question of his painterly skill, this action
of the knife reproduced, as nothing else could, the action of a
stream of light passing over the broken surface of leaves,
rock, grass, a stream of light which confers life and
conviction but does not necessarily reveal structure.

Correspondences like these suggest an intimate
relationship between Courbet's practice as a painter and the
countryside in which he grew up. But they do not in
themselves answer the question of what *meaning* he gave to
appearances. We need to interrogate the landscape further.
Rocks are the primary configuration of this landscape. They
bestow identity, allow focus. It is the outcrops of rock which
create the presence of the landscape. Allowing the term its
full resonance, one can talk about *rock faces*. The rocks are
the character, the spirit of the region. Proudhon, who came
from the same area, wrote: "I am pure Jurassic limestone."
Courbet, boastful as always, said that in his paintings, "I
even make stones think."

A rockface is always there. (Think of the Louvre
landscape which is called *The ten o'clock road*). It dominates
and demands to be seen, yet its appearance, in both form
and colour, changes according to light and weather. It
continually offers different facets of itself to visibility.
Compared to a tree, an animal, a person, its appearances
are only very weakly normative. A rock can look like almost
anything. It is undeniably itself, and yet its substance does
not posit any particular form. It emphatically exists and yet
its appearance (within a few very broad geological
limitations) is arbitrary. It is only like it is, this time. Its
appearance is, in fact, the limit of its meaning.

To grow up surrounded by such rocks is to grow up in a

region in which the visible is both lawless and irreduceably real. There is visual fact but a minimum of visual order. Courbet, according to his friend Francis Wey, was able to paint an object convincingly — say a distant pile of cut wood — *without knowing what it was.* That is unusual amongst painters, and it is, I think, very significant.

In the early romantic *Self-portrait with a dog,* he painted himself, surrounded by the darkness of his cape and hat, against a large boulder. And there his own face and hand are painted in exactly the same spirit as the stone behind. They were comparable visual phenomena, possessing the same visual reality. If visibility is lawless, there is no hierarchy of appearances. Courbet painted everything — snow, flesh, hair, fur, clothes, bark — as he would have painted it had it been a rock face. Nothing he painted has interiority — not even, amazingly, his copy of a Rembrandt self-portrait — but everything is depicted with amazement: amazement because to see, where there are no laws, is to be constantly surprised.

It may now seem that I am treating Courbet as if he were "timeless," as unhistorical as the Jura mountains which so influenced him. This is not my intention. The landscape of the Jura influenced his painting in the way that it did, given the historical situation in which he was working as a painter, and given his specific temperament. Even by the standards of Jurassic time, the Jura will have "produced" only one Courbet. The "geographical interpretation" does no more than ground, give material, visual substance to, the social-historical one.

It is hard to summarize Timothy Clark's percipient and subtle research on Courbet in a few sentences. He allows us to see the political period in all its complexity. He places the legends that surrounded the painter: the legend of the country buffoon with a gift for the paintbrush; the legend of the dangerous revolutionary; the legend of the coarse, drunken, thigh-slapping provocateur. (Probably the truest and most sympathetic portrait of Courbet is by Jules Valles in his *Cri du Peuple*).

And then Clark shows how in fact in the great works of the early 1850s Courbet, with his inordinate ambition, with his genuine hatred of the bourgeoisie, with his rural experience, with his love of the theatrical, and with an extraordinary intuition, was engaged in nothing less than a double transformation of the art of painting. Double because it proposed a transformation of subject matter and audience. For a few years he was able to work, inspired by the ideal of both becoming popular for the first time.

The transformation involved "capturing" painting as it was and altering its address. One can think of Courbet, I believe, as the last master. He learnt his prodigious skill in handling paint from the Venetians, from Rembrandt, from Velasquez, from Zurbaran and others. As a practitioner he remained traditionalist. Yet he acquired the skills he did, without taking over the traditional values which those skills had been designed to serve. One might say he stole his professionalism.

For example: the practice of nude painting was closely associated with values of tact, luxury and wealth. The nude was an erotic ornament. Courbet stole the practice of the nude and used it to depict the "vulgar" nakedness of a countrywoman with her clothes in a heap on a river bank. (Later, as disillusion set in — he too produced erotic ornaments like *The woman with a parrot*).

For example: the practice of 17th century Spanish realism was closely connected with the religious principle of the moral value of simplicity and austerity and the dignity of charity. Courbet stole the practice and used it in *The stonebreakers* to present desperate unredeemed rural poverty.

139

For example: the Dutch 17th century practice of painting group portraits was a way of celebrating a certain *esprit de corps*. Courbet stole the practice for the *Burial at Ornans* to reveal a mass solitude in face of the grave.

The hunter from the Jura, the rural democrat and the bandit painter came together in the same artist for a few years between 1848 and 1856 to produce some shocking and unique images. For all three personae, appearances were a direct experience, relatively unmediated by convention, and for that very reason astounding and unpredictable. The vision of all three was both matter-of-fact (termed by his opponents *vulgar*) and innocent (termed by his opponents *stupid*). After 1856, during the debauch of the Second Empire, it was only the hunter who sometimes produced landscapes which were still unlike those by any other painter, landscapes on which snow might settle.

In the *Burial* of 1849-50 we can glimpse something of the soul of Courbet, the single soul which, at different moments, was hunter, democrat and bandit painter. Despite his appetite for life, his bragging and proverbial laughter, Courbet's view of life was probably sombre if not tragic.

Along the middle of the canvas, for its whole length (nearly seven yards), runs a zone of darkness, of black. Nominally this black can be explained by the clothes of the massed mourners. But it is too pervasive and too deep — even allowing for the fact that over the years the whole painting has darkened — for its significance to stop there. It is the dark of the valley landscape, of the approaching night and of the earth into which the coffin will be placed. Yet I think this darkness also had a social and personal significance.

Emerging from the zone of darkness are the faces of Courbet's family, friends and acquaintances at Ornans, painted without idealisation and without rancour, painted without recourse to a pre-established norm. The painting was called cynical, sacrilegious, brutish. It was treated as if it were a plot. Yet what was involved in the plot? A cult of the ugly? Social subversion? An attack on the church? The critics searched the painting in vain to discover clues. Nobody discovered the source of its actual subversion.

Courbet had painted a group of men and women as they might appear when attending a village funeral, and he had refused to organise (harmonise) these appearances into some false — or even true — higher meaning. He had refused the function of art as the moderator of appearances, as that which ennobles the visible. Instead, he had painted life-size, on 21 square metres of canvas, an assembly of figures at a graveside, which announced *nothing* except: This is how we appear. And precisely to the degree to which the art public in Paris received this announcement from the countryside, they denied its truth, calling it vicious exaggeration.

In his soul Courbet may have foreseen this; his grandiose hopes were perhaps a device for giving him the courage to continue. The insistence with which he painted — in the *Burial,* in *The stonebreakers,* in *The peasants of Flagey,* whatever emerged into the light, insisting on every apparent part as equally valuable, leads me to think that the ground of darkness signified entrenched ignorance. When he said that art "is the most *complete* expression of an existing thing," he was opposing art to any hierarchical system or to any culture whose function is to diminish or deny the expression of a large part of what exists. He was the only great painter to challenge the chosen ignorance of the cultured.

1978

141

Turner and the Barber's Shop

There has never been another painter like Turner. And this is because he combined in his work so many different elements. There is a strong argument for claiming that it is Turner, not Dickens or Wordsworth or Walter Scott or Constable or Landseer, who, in his genius, represents most fully the character of the British 19th century. And it may be this which explains the fact that Turner is the only important artist who both before and after his death in 1851 had a certain popular appeal in Britain. Until recently a wide public felt that somehow, mysteriously, dumbly (in the sense that his vision dismisses or precludes words), Turner was expressing something of the bedrock of their own varied experience.

Turner was born in 1775, the son of a back-street barber in central London. His uncle was a butcher. The family lived a stone's throw from the Thames. During his life Turner travelled a great deal, but in most of his chosen themes water, coastlines, or river banks recur continually. During the last years of his life he lived — under the alias of Captain Booth, a retired sea captain — a little further down the river at Chelsea. During his middle years he lived at Hammersmith and Twickenham, both overlooking the Thames.

He was a child prodigy and by the age of nine he was already earning money by colouring engravings; at fourteen he entered the Royal Academy Schools. When he was eighteen he had his own studio, and shortly afterwards his father gave up his trade to become his son's studio assistant and factotum. The relation between father and son was obviously close. (The painter's mother died insane.)

It is impossible to know exactly what early visual experiences affected Turner's imagination. But there is a strong correspondence between some of the visual elements of a barber's shop and the elements of the painter's mature style, which should be noticed in passing without being used as a comprehensive explanation. Consider some of his later paintings and imagine, in the backstreet shop, water, froth, steam, gleaming metal, clouded mirrors, white bowls or basins in which soapy liquid is agitated by the barber's brush and detritus deposited. Consider the equivalence between his father's razor and the palette knife which, despite criticisms and current usage, Turner insisted upon using so extensively. More profoundly — at the level of childish phantasmagoria — picture the always possible combination, suggested by a barber's shop, of blood and water, water and blood. At the age of twenty Turner planned to paint a subject from the Apocalypse entitled: *The Water Turned to Blood.* He never painted it. But visually, by way of sunsets and fires, it became the subject of thousands of his later works and studies.

Many of Turner's earlier landscapes were more or less classical, referring back to Claude Lorrain, but influenced also by the first Dutch landscapists. The spirit of these works is curious. On the face of it, they are calm, "sublime," or gently nostalgic. Eventually, however, one realizes that these landscapes have far more to do with art than nature, and that as art they are a form of pastiche. And in pastiche there is always a kind of restlessness or desperation.

Nature entered Turner's work — or rather his imagination — as violence. As early as 1802 he painted a storm raging round the jetty at Calais. Soon afterwards he painted another storm in the Alps. Then an avalanche. Until the 1830s the two aspects of his work, the apparently calm and the turbulent, existed side by side, but gradually the turbulence became more and more dominant. In the end violence was implicit in Turner's vision itself; it no longer depended upon the subject. For example, the painting entitled *Peace: Burial at Sea* is, in its own way, as violent as the painting of *The Snowstorm*. The former is like an image of a wound being cauterized.

The violence in Turner's paintings appears to be elemental: it is expressed by water, by wind, by fire. Sometimes it appears to be a quality which belongs just to the light. Writing about a late painting called *The Angel Standing in the Sun,* Turner spoke of light *devouring* the whole visible world. Yet I believe that the violence he found in nature only acted as a confirmation of something intrinsic to his own imaginative vision. I have already suggested how this vision may have been partly born from childhood experience. Later it would have been confirmed, not only by nature, but by human enterprise. Turner lived through the first apocalyptic phase of the British Industrial Revolution. Steam meant more than what filled a barber's shop. Vermilion meant furnaces as well as blood. Wind whistled through valves as well as over the Alps. The light which he thought of as devouring the whole visible world was very similar to the new productive energy which was challenging and destroying all previous ideas about wealth, distance, human labour, the city, nature, the will of God, children, time. It is a mistake to think of Turner as a virtuoso painter of natural effects — which was more or less how he was officially estimated until Ruskin interpreted his work more deeply.

The first half of the British 19th century was profoundly unreligious. This may have forced Turner to use nature symbolically. No other convincing or accessible system of symbolism made a deep moral appeal, but its moral sense could not be expressed directly. The *Burial at Sea* shows the burial of the painter, Sir David Wilkie, who was one of Turner's few friends. Its references are cosmic. But as a statement, is it essentially a protest or an acceptance? Do we take more account of the impossibly black sails or of the impossibly radiant city beyond? The questions raised by the painting are moral — hence, as in many of Turner's later works, its somewhat claustrophobic quality — but the answers given are all ambivalent. No wonder that what Turner admired in painting was the ability to cast doubt, to throw into mystery. Rembrandt, he said admiringly, "threw a mysterious doubt over the meanest piece of common."

From the outset of his career Turner was extremely ambitious in an undisguisedly competitive manner. He wanted to be recognized not only as the greatest painter of his country and time, but among the greatest of all time. He saw himself as the equal of Rembrandt and Watteau. He believed that he had outpainted Claude Lorrain. This competitiveness was accompanied by a marked tendency towards misanthropy and miserliness. He was excessively secretive about his working methods. He was a recluse in the sense that he lived apart from society by choice. His solitariness was not a by-product of neglect or lack of recognition. From an early age his career was a highly successful one. As his work became more original, it was criticized. Sometimes his solitary eccentricity was called madness; but he was never treated as being less than a great painter.

He wrote poetry on the themes of his paintings, he wrote and sometimes delivered lectures on art, in both cases using a grandiloquent but vapid language. In conversation he was taciturn and rough. If one says that he was a visionary, one must qualify it by emphasizing hardheaded empiricism. He preferred to live alone, but he saw to it that he succeeded in a highly competitive society. He had grandiose visions which achieved greatness when he painted them and were merely bombastic when he wrote about them, yet his most serious conscious attitude as an artist was pragmatic and almost artisanal: what drew him to a subject or a particular painting device was what he called its *practicability* — its capacity to yield a painting.

Turner's genius was of a new type which was called forth by the British 19th century, but more usually in the field of science or engineering or business. (Somewhat later the same type appeared as hero in the United States.) He had the ability to be highly successful, but success did not satisfy him. (He left a fortune of £140,000.) He felt himself to be alone in history. He had global visions which words were inadequate to express and which could only be presented under the pretext of a *practical* production. He visualized man as being dwarfed by immense forces over which he had no control but which nevertheless he had discovered. He was close to despair, and yet he was sustained by an extraordinary productive energy, (In his studio after his death there were 19,000 drawings and watercolours and several hundred oil paintings.)

Ruskin wrote that Turner's underlying theme was Death. I believe rather that it was solitude and violence and the impossibility of redemption. Most of his paintings are as if about the aftermath of crime. And what is so disturbing about them — what actually allows them to be seen as beautiful — is not the guilt but the global indifference that they record.

On a few notable occasions during his life Turner was able to express his visions through actual incidents which he witnessed. In October, 1834, the Houses of Parliament caught fire. Turner rushed to the scene, made furious sketches and produced the finished painting for the Royal Academy the following year. Several years later, when he was sixty-six years old, he was on a steamboat in a snow storm and afterwards painted the experience. Whenever a painting was based on a real event he emphasized, in the title or in his catalogue notes, that the work was the result of first hand experience. It was as though he wished to prove that life — however remorselessly — confirmed his vision. The full title of *The Snowstorm* was *Snowstorm. Steamboat off a Harbour's Mouth Making Signals in Shallow Water, and going by the Lead. The Author was in this storm on the night the Ariel left Harwich.*

When a friend informed Turner that his mother had liked the snowstorm painting, Turner remarked: "I did not paint it to be understood, but I wished to show what such a scene was like: I got sailors to lash me to the mast to observe it; I was lashed for four hours, and I did not expect to escape, but I felt bound to record it if I did. But no one had any business to like the picture."

"But my mother went through just such a scene, and it brought it all back to her."

"Is your mother a painter?"

"No."

"Then she ought to have been thinking of something else."

The question remains what made these works, likeable or not, so new, so different. Turner transcended the principle of traditional landscape: the principle that a landscape is something which unfolds before you. In *The Burning of the Houses of Parliament* the scene begins to extend beyond its formal edges. It begins to work its way round the spectator in an effort to outflank and surround him. In *The Snowstorm* the tendency has become fact. If one really allows one's eye to be absorbed into the forms and colours on the canvas, one begins to realize that, looking at it, one is in the centre of a maelstrom: there is no longer a near and a far. For example, the lurch into the distance is not, as one would expect, *into*

147

the picture, but out of it towards the right-hand edge. It is a picture which precludes the outsider spectator.

Turner's physical courage must have been considerable. His courage as an artist before his own experience was perhaps even greater. His truthfulness to that experience was such that he destroyed the tradition to which he was so proud to belong. He stopped painting totalities. *The Snowstorm* is the total of everything which can be seen and grasped by the man tied to the mast of that ship. There is *nothing* outside it. This makes the idea of anyone liking it absurd.

Perhaps Turner did not think exactly in these terms. But he followed intuitively the logic of the situation. He was a man alone, surrounded by implacable and indifferent forces. It was no longer possible to believe that what he saw could ever be seen from the outside — even though this would have been a consolation. Parts could no longer be treated as wholes. There was either nothing or everything.

In a more practical sense he was aware of the importance of totality in his life's work. He became reluctant to sell his paintings. He wanted as many of his pictures as possible to be kept together, and he became obsessed by the idea of bequeathing them to the nation so that they could be exhibited as a whole. "Keep them together," he said. "What is the use of them but together?" Why? Because only then might they conceivably bear obstinate witness to his experience for which, he believed, there was no precedent and no great hope of future understanding.

1972.

Rouault and the Suburbs of Paris

"I have been so happy painting, a fool who paints, forgetting everything in the blackest gloom." This is one of the many remarks which Georges Rouault made about himself. Like his art, it is apparently simple, in fact contradictory (how is one *happy* forgetting everything in the *blackest gloom?*) and authentically desperate.

He was a short man of 5 feet 6 inches. Versions of his own face are to be found in several of his clown paintings. Yet in reality Rouault's face was thinner skinned and both more receptive and more malicious than those of his painted clowns. It was a nocturnal, solitary face. One might have rashly concluded from his photograph that he was an aberrant entomologist obsessed by moths.

He was born in Paris in May, 1871, when the city was being shelled by government troops, just before they entered and began their massacres. His father was a cabinetmaker. The suburbs of Paris where he was brought up were to supply him with the setting and the atmosphere of many of his paintings and etchings. There are many different aspects of the suburbs of Paris and different ways of seeing them. Rouault's suburbs have little to do with those of the Impressionists or of Utrillo. His are the suburbs of the long road leading away, of dim street lamps at dusk, of lonely itinerants and of those who have failed in the city but are forced to stay on its fringes. There are no precise landmarks of these suburbs in Rouault's paintings. What they constitute is a spiritual climate — probably the climate of his own youth. He himself called one such work *The Suburb of Long Suffering.*

At the age of fourteen he became an apprentice to a stained glass maker and attended art classes in the evening. Critics have made much of the influence of stained glass on his art, citing particularly his luminous colours and his heavy black outlines like the lead in stained glass windows. The resemblance is indeed close, but in my opinion it does not explain much. The essence of Rouault's art is psychological, not stylistic.

When he was nineteen he became the pupil of Gustave Moreau and began to paint dark mysterious landscapes and religious subjects in that nineteenth-century Romantic manner which it was believed followed in the footsteps of Rembrandt. They seem, these pictures, like images imagined in the folds of heavy hanging curtains. Pupil and master became deeply attached to each other. "My poor Rouault," Moreau said to him, "I can read your future. With your absolute single-mindedness, your passion for work, your love of the unusual in paint structures — all your essential qualities, in fact — you will be more and more a figure on your own."

In 1898, Moreau died. The shock and the ensuing solitude projected Rouault, frenzied, beside himself, into the great creative period of his life.

"My feelings at Moreau's death were heartbreaking, but after being completely overwhelmed at first, I was not long in reacting, and it was an extremely profound inner change. I had just won a medal at the Salon and I could have built up a very comfortable position in official circles; I also had steady contacts with Moreau's admirers.

"But you have to suffer and see for yourself, my master used to say, and it was no merit of mine to do so; there was nothing else I could do. Without deliberately wanting to forget all I had loved in the museums, I was gradually carried away by a more objective vision.

"It was then that I passed through a most violent moral crisis. I experienced things that cannot be put into words.

And I set about doing painting of an outrageous lyricism which disconcerted everybody.

"For many years I wonder how I lived. Everybody dropped me, in spite of elegant, but vain, protests. People even wrote letters of abuse. That was the time to remember the words of my master: 'Thank heaven that you are not successful, at least until as late as possible. That way you can express yourself more completely, and without constraint.'

"But when I looked at some of my pictures, I asked myself, was it really I who painted that? Can it be true? It is frightening what I have done."

What had he done? Death had made life real and at the same time hateful to him. He went out into the streets, the waste lots, the law courts, the cabarets, the public institutions of the city and painted those he saw there. He painted hucksters, judges, prostitutes, rent collectors, bons vivants, teachers, circus performers, wives, butchers, barristers, criminals, lecturers, tradesmen. Some he hated for themselves. The victims aroused his hatred of those who had wronged them. He painted on scraps of paper with an eccentric mixture of materials: watercolour, gouache, pastel, oil paint, ink. This may at first have been due to his poverty — he had to use whatever was at hand; but his intemperate use of material on top of material corresponded also to the paroxysmal nature of his vision.

He had descended into what he thought was hell. Hell was established for him by the people he encountered there and their uses of each other, but it was established no less by his awareness of his own intransigence and the power of his own hatred. He was himself permeated by the outrages and sins among which he found himself. But unlike Baudelaire, whom he admired, he could never place himself in the position of another. Rouault remains at all times the one who records and condemns.

This is very clear in, for example, a painting of a prostitute sitting before the mirror. Describing such prostitutes who posed for him, Rouault wrote of their "thick gelatinous masses of flesh, vacillating flesh, upon which no genuine kiss will ever again be pressed." Today these paintings are said to illustrate the vanity of the flesh, the bitter truths of ageing, the bleakness of promiscuity. But if you look more carefully at the picture, it is evidence of something quite different. What degrades the woman sitting there are the black lines with which Rouault has outlined and interpreted her. The slash between the breasts. The burnt holes of the eyes. Remove these black marks in your imagination and you are left with a not unattractive woman whose nakedness is ambiguous. You are still seeing through Rouault's eyes: but what you see no longer corresponds to the disgust of his verbal description because you have removed the stigma of his misanthropy and you are seeing the woman as he would have perceived her if he had not already decided that "no genuine" kiss would ever again be pressed upon her, and that, therefore, he was obliged to press on her nakedness his own judgment of the world.

A work like this is born of a vision which condemns the world *a priori*. The judgment does not arise out of what it shows; on the contrary, what it shows has been sought in order to confirm the judgment. Yet as an artist Rouault worked in good faith, for these images, if one looks at them with open eyes, reveal the truth about their own motivation. No other artist has ever produced such a volume of purely misanthropic work as Rouault during the period between 1905 and 1912. These pictures record the tragedy of their own vision. Confronted with the head of the scourged Christ, you see the lines and slashes and black marks of his paint confessing to their own cruelty.

In 1912, a second death deeply affected Rouault, this time that of his father.

"We are all refugees in this life. Refugees from illness, from boredom, from nethermost poverty, from friendlessness, from the whisper of scandal, from death above all. We hide ourselves under the sheets, pulling them up to our chins with a shaky hand, and even at the moment of going under we are still talking — talking of retirement, and of taking our ease among the Borromean Isles in Italy."

His painting gradually changed. Some of his subjects remained the same — clowns, dwarfs, judges. The new painting was no less sombre in spirit. But it was resonant in colour and it increasingly referred to another hieratic, introspective, sacred world where there was no place for hatred but only contrition. The black lines and stains of paint changed their function. Instead of condemning, they register static accepted suffering.

It is as though in his new work Rouault paints from within a church. His work is not conventional religious art, nor is it Catholic propaganda. The point I am making is only in terms of Rouault's own personal psychic development. From about 1914 onwards, most of his paintings are images conceived as altarpieces. They continually refer back to the period from 1905 to 1912, but they do so in something like a spirit of atonement. Is it to atone for his earlier work, one asks oneself, that he is now there alone in the church?

No life is as simple as the answer to a direct question like that. But the rest of Rouault's story does suggest a tortuous, guilt-ridden attitude to his own creative past.

In 1917, the art dealer Vollard bought up Rouault's entire output, which then consisted of nearly 800 paintings, many of them belonging to the period of 1905-1912. Rouault claimed that most of these paintings were unfinished, and he made Vollard agree that he would sell no work until the painter declared it finished. During the following thirty years of his working life, Rouault saw himself as the prisoner of his contract, bound to the impossible of finishing to his own satisfaction what was already completed. "Atlas bearing the world on his shoulders," he wrote, "is a child compared to me . . . it is killing me . . . the whole of my effort, past, present and future, is at stake with Ambroise Vollard. That is why I exhaust myself with sleepless nights, why I pray in secret, it is perhaps why I shall succumb."

Vollard was killed in an accident in 1939. The news of his death in no way came as a release to Rouault. Once again he was stricken. But after the war he brought a legal case against Vollard's heirs and demanded the return of his unfinished works. He won the case. His old paintings passed into his hands. On November 5, 1948, he publicly burned 315 of them because he believed that he could never finish them, never render them acceptable to his own conscience and the world.

1972

Magritte and the Impossible

Magritte accepts and uses a certain language of painting. This language is over 500 years old and its first master was Van Eyck. It assumes that the truth is to be found in appearances which are therefore worth preserving by being represented. It assumes continuity in time as also in space. It is a language which treats, most naturally, of *objects* — furniture, glass, fabrics, houses. It is capable of expressing spiritual experience but always within a concrete setting, always circumscribed by a certain static materiality — its human figures were like miraculous statues. This value of materiality was expressed through the illusion of tangibility. I cannot trace here the transformation which this language underwent during five centuries. But its essential assumptions remained unchanged and form part of what most Europeans still expect from the visual arts: likeness, the representation of appearances, the depiction of particular events and their settings.

Magritte never questioned the aptness of this language for expressing what he had to say. Thus there is no obscurity in his art. Everything is plainly readable. Even in his early work when he was far less skillful than he became during the last twenty years of his life. (I use the word *readable* metaphorically: his language is visual, not literary, though being a language, it signifies something other than itself.) Yet what he had to say destroyed the *raison-d'être* of the language he used; the point of most of his paintings depends on what is *not* shown, upon the event that is *not* taking place, upon what can *dis*appear.

Let us examine some early examples: *L'Assassin menacé*. The assassin stands listening to a record on a gramophone. Two plain-clothes policemen wait behind corners to arrest him. A woman lies dead. Through the window three men

155

stare at the murderer's back. We are shown everything —
and nothing. We see a particular event in its concrete
setting, yet everything remains mysterious — the committed
murder, the future arrest, the appearance of the three
staring men in the window. What fills the depicted moment
is the sound of the record, and this, by the very nature of
painting, we cannot hear. (Magritte frequently uses the idea
of sound to comment upon the limitation of the visual.)

Another early painting: *La Femme Introuvable*. It shows a
number of irregular stones embedded in cement. These
stones frame a nude woman and four large hands searching
for her. The painting stresses the quality of tangibility. Yet
although the hands can feel their way over the stones, the
woman eludes them.

A third early painting is called *Le Musée d'une nuit*. It
depicts four cupboard shelves. An apple lies on one shelf, a
severed hand on the second, and a piece of lead on the third.
Over the fourth opening is stuck a piece of pink paper with
scissor-cut holes in it. Through the holes we see nothing but
darkness. Yet we assume that the significant, the all-
revealing exhibit of the night lies behind the paper on the
fourth shelf.

A year later Magritte painted a smoker's pipe, and on the
canvas beneath the pipe he wrote: *"Ceci n'est pas une pipe."*
He made two languages (the visual and the verbal) cancel
one another out.

What does this continual cancelling out mean? Despite
Magritte's warnings to the contrary, critics have tended to
interpret his work symbolically and to romanticise its
mystery. He himself said that his pictures should be thought
of "as material signs of the freedom of thought." And he
defined what he meant by this freedom: "Life, the
Universe, the Void, have no value for thought when it is
truly free. The only thing that has value for it is Meaning,

156

that is the moral concept of the Impossible.''

To conceive of the impossible is difficult. Magritte knew this. ''In both the ordinary and extraordinary moments of life, our thought does not manifest its freedom to its fullest extent. It is unceasingly threatened or involved in what happens to us. It *coincides* with a thousand and one things which restrict it. This coincidence is almost permanent.'' Almost, but the experience of escaping from it occurs spontaneously and briefly some time or another in most lives.

First, let us judge Magritte's work in the light of his own aims. This means that we should decide in each case how cleanly he has broken free of the contingent and coincidental. His links with the surrealist movement and that movement's rather vague appeals to the unconscious and the automatic have previously confused this issue.

There are paintings by Magritte which do not get beyond expressing a *sensation* of the impossible such as we experience in dreams or states of half-consciousness. Such sensations isolate us from the coincidental, but do not liberate us from it. I would cite as examples his paintings of the gigantic apple which fills an entire room *(La Chambre d'écoute)* or many of the paintings of the early 1950s in which figures or whole scenes have been turned to stone. By contrast, his fully successful paintings are those in which the impossible has been grasped, measured and inserted as an *absence* in a statement made in a language originally and specially developed for depicting particular events in particular settings. Such paintings *(Le Modèle rouge, Le Voyageur, Au Seuil de la liberté)* are triumphs of Magritte's Meaning, triumphs of the moral concept of the Impossible.

If a painting by Magritte confirms one's lived experience to date, it has by his standards, failed; if it temporarily destroys that experience, it has succeeded. (This destruction is the only fearful thing in his art.) The paradox of his art and of his insight was that to destroy familiar experience he needed to use the language of the familiar. Unlike most modern artists he despised the exotic. He hated the familiar and the ordinary too much to turn his back on them.

Were his aims valid? What is the value of his art for its public?

Max Raphael wrote that the aim of all art was "the undoing of the world of things" and the establishment of a world of values. Marcuse refers to art as "the great refusal" of the world as it is. I myself have written that art mediates between what is given and what is desired. Yet the great works of the past, in their opposition to what was, were able to believe in a language and to refer to established sets of values. The contradiction between what was and what could be thought was not yet insurmountable. Hence the unity achieved in their works. Indeed their critique of a disparate reality (whether one thinks of Piero, Rembrandt, Poussin or Cézanne) was always in the name of a greater and more profound unity. In this century — and more precisely since 1941 — the contradiction has become insurmountable, unity in a work of art inconceivable. Our idea of freedom extends, our experience of it diminishes. It is from this that the moral concept of the Impossible arises. Only through the occasional interstices of the interlocking oppressive systems can we glimpse the impossibility of it being otherwise: an impossibility which inspires us because we know that the optimum of what is considered possible within these systems is inadequate.

"I am not a determinist," wrote Magritte, "but I don't believe in chance either. It serves as still another 'explanation' of the world. The problem lies precisely in not accepting any explanation of the world either through chance or determinism. I am not responsible for my belief. It is not even I who decides that I am not responsible — and so on to infinity: I am obliged not to believe. There is no point of departure''.

This statement — as always with Magritte — is remarkable for its clarity. But what it describes is part of the lived experience of millions. It is perhaps the conclusion of the majority in the industrialised countries. Who has not been forced at some time or another to the intransigent helplessness of this attitude? Magritte the artist, however, continues from where the statement ends. There is such a thing as a reduction, not to absurdity, but to freedom. Magritte's best, most eloquent, paintings are about this reduction. *Le Modèle rouge* shows a pair of boots of which the toes have become human toes, placed on the ground in front of a wooden wall. I do not wish to impose a single meaning on any of Magritte's paintings, but I am sure that invention of the boots-half-turned-into-feet is not the point of this painting. This would be mystery for mystery's sake, which he hated. The point is what possibility/impossibility does such an invention propose? An ordinary pair of boots left on the ground would simply suggest that somebody had taken them off. A pair of severed feet would suggest violence. But the discarded feet-half-turned-into-boots propose the notion of a self that has left its own skin. The painting is about what is absent, about a freedom that *is* absence.

Les Promenades d'Euclide shows a window overlooking a town. In front of the window is an easel with a canvas on it. What is painted on the canvas coincides exactly with that part of the townscape which it covers. There is a second pun. The piece of landscape painted upon (or covered by?) the canvas includes a straight road going as far as the horizon and, beside it, a pointed tower.

The road in perspective and the tower are the same size, colour and pointed shape. The purpose of the puns is to demonstrate how easy it is to confuse the two-dimensional with the three-dimensional, surface with substance. And so we come to the proposition. The easel has a handle by turning which the canvas is lowered or raised. Magritte has painted this handle very tangibly and emphatically. What will happen if it is turned? Is it possible/impossible that when the canvas moves, we shall see that behind where it originally was *there is no landscape at all:* nothing, a free blank? Another painting, *La Lunette d'approche,* makes the same proposition. We see a double window with one of its frames not quite shut. On or through the glass of the windows is a conventional sunlit sea and sky. But through the gap behind the appearances of the sea and sky we glimpse a free dark impossible emptiness.

L'Evidence éternelle. This work consists of five separate framed canvases each depicting a close-up of a part of the same woman; her hand, her breasts, her stomach and sex, her knees, her feet. Together they offer visible evidence of her body and of her physical proximity. Yet how much is this evidence worth? Any one of the parts can be removed or they can be arranged in a different order. The work proposes that what appears to exist — the *res extensa* — may be seen as a series of discontinuous movable parts. *Behind* the parts and *through* their interstices we imagine an impossible freedom.

When the cannon fires, in his painting *On The Threshold of Liberty,* the panels of the apparent world will fall down.

Magritte's work derives from a profound social and cultural crisis which will probably continue to make any unified art impossible this side of several revolutions. His work might be said to be defeatist.

Nevertheless he refused to retreat from the present as it is lived, by way of a cult of either aesthetics or personality. What he had to make as an artist, he made of the present. This is why very many can recognise in Magritte a part of

160

themselves which otherwise has no place in the present; the part which cannot concur with the rest of their lives, which cannot refute the moral concept of the impossible, which is the product of the violence done to the other parts.

1969

Hals and Bankruptcy

In my mind's eye I see the story of Frans Hals in theatrical terms.

The first act opens with a banquet that has already been going on for several hours. (In reality these banquets often continued for several days.) It is a banquet for the officers of one of the civic guard companies of Haarlem — let us say the St George's Company of 1627. I choose this one because Hals's painted record of the occasion is the greatest of his civic guard group portraits.

The officers are gay, noisy and emphatic. Their soldierly air has more to do with the absence of women and with their uniforms than with their faces or gestures, which are too bland for campaigning soldiers. And on second thoughts even their uniforms seem curiously unworn. The toasts which they drink to one another are to eternal friendship and trust. May all prosper together!

One of the most animated is Captain Michiel de Wael — down-stage wearing a yellow jerkin. The look on his face is the look of a man certain that he is as young as the night and certain that all his companions can see it. It is a look that you can find at a certain moment at most tables in any night-club. But before Hals it had never been recorded. We watch Captain de Wael as the sober always watch a man getting tipsy — coldly and very aware of being an outsider. It is like watching a departure for a journey we haven't the means to make. Twelve years later Hals painted the same man wearing the same chamois jerkin at another banquet. The stare, the look, has become fixed and the eyes wetter. If he can, he now spends the afternoons drinking at club bars. And his throaty voice as he talks and tells stories has a kind of urgency which hints that once, a long way back when he was young, he lived as we have never done.

Hals is at the banquet — though not in the painting. He is a man of nearly fifty, also drinking heavily. He is at the height of his success. He has the reputation of being wilful and alternately lethargic and violent. (Twenty years ago there was a scandal because they said he beat his wife to death when drunk. Afterwards he married again and had eight children.) He is a man of very considerable intelligence. We have no evidence about his conversation but I am certain that it was quick, epigrammatic, critical. Part of his attraction must have lain in the fact that he behaved as though he actually enjoyed the freedom which his companions believed in in principle. His even greater attraction was in his incomparable ability as a painter. Only he could paint his companions as they wished. Only he could bridge the contradiction in their wish. Each must be painted as a distinct individual and, at the same time, as a spontaneous natural member of the group.

Who are these men? As we sensed, they are not soldiers. The civic guards, although originally formed for active service, have long since become purely ceremonial clubs. These men come from the richest and most powerful merchant families in Haarlem, which is a textile-manufacturing centre.

Haarlem is only eleven miles from Amsterdam and twenty years before, Amsterdam had suddenly and spectacularly become the financial capital of the entire world. Speculation concerning grain, precious metals, currencies, slaves, spices and commodities of every kind is being pursued on a scale and with a success that leaves the rest of Europe not only amazed but dependent on Dutch capital.

A new energy has been released and a kind of metaphysic of money is being born. Money acquires its own virtue — and, on its own terms, demonstrates its own tolerance.

(Holland is the only state in Europe without religious persecution.) All traditional values are being either superseded or placed within limits and so robbed of their absolutism. The States of Holland have officially declared that the Church has no concern with questions of usury within the world of banking. Dutch arms-merchants consistently sell arms, not only to every contestant in Europe, but also, during the cruellest wars, to their own enemies.

The officers of the St George's Company of the Haarlem Civic Guard belong to the first generation of the modern spirit of Free Enterprise. A little later Hals painted a portrait which seems to me to depict this spirit more vividly than any other painting or photograph I have ever seen. It is of Willem van Heythuyzen.

What distinguishes this portrait from all earlier portraits of wealthy or powerful men is its instability. Nothing is secure in its place. You have the feeling of looking at a man in a ship's cabin during a gale. The table will slide across the floor. The book will fall off the table. The curtain will tumble down.

Furthermore, to emphasize and make a virtue out of this precariousness, the man leans back on his chair to the maximum angle of possible balance, and tenses the switch which he is holding in his hands so as almost to make it snap. And it is the same with his face and expression. His glance is a momentary one, and around his eyes you see the tiredness which is the consequence of having always, at each moment, to calculate afresh.

At the same time the portrait in no way suggests decay or disintegration. There may be a gale but the ship is sailing fast and confidently. Today van Heythuyzen would doubtless be described by his associates as being 'electric', and there are millions who model themselves — though not necessarily consciously — on the bearing of such men.

Put van Heythuyzen in a swivel chair, without altering his posture, pull the desk up in front of him, change the switch in his hands to a ruler or an aluminium rod, and he becomes a typical modern executive, sparing a few moments of his time to listen to your case.

But to return to the banquet. All the men are now somewhat drunk. The hands that previously balanced a knife, held a glass between two fingers, or squeezed a lemon over the oysters, now fumble a little. At the same time their gestures become more exaggerated — and more directed towards us, the imaginary audience. There is nothing like alcohol for making one believe that the self one is presenting is one's true, up to now always hidden, self.

They interrupt each other and talk at cross-purposes. The less they communicate by thought, the more they put their arms round each other. From time to time they sing, content that at last they are acting in unison, for each, half lost in his own fantasy of self-presentation, wishes to prove to himself and to the others only one thing — that he is the truest friend there.

Hals is more often than not a little apart from the group. And he appears to be watching them as we are watching them.

The second act opens on the same set with the same banqueting table, but now Hals sits alone at the end of it. He is in his late sixties or early seventies, but still very much in possession of his faculties. The passing of the intervening years has, however, considerably changed the atmosphere of the scene. It has acquired a curiously mid-nineteenth-century air. Hals is dressed in a black cloak, with a black hat somewhat like a nineteenth-century top hat. The bottle in front of him is black. The only relief to the blackness is his loose white collar and the white page of the book open on the table.

The blackness, however, is not funereal. It has a rakish and defiant quality about it. We think of Baudelaire. We begin to understand why Courbet and Manet admired Hals so much.

The turning point occurred in 1645. For several years before that, Hals had received fewer and fewer commissions. The spontaneity of his portraits which had so pleased his contemporaries became unfashionable with the next generation, who already wanted portraits which were more morally reassuring — who demanded in fact the prototypes of that official bourgeois hypocritical portraiture which has gone on ever since.

In 1645 Hals painted a portrait of a man in black looking over the back of a chair. Probably the sitter was a friend. His expression is another one that Hals was the first to record. It is the look of a man who does not believe in the life he witnesses, yet can see no alternative. He has considered, quite impersonally, the possibility that life may be absurd. He is by no means desperate. He is interested. But his intelligence isolates him from the current purpose of men and the supposed purpose of God. A few years later Hals painted a self-portrait displaying a different character but the same expression.

As he sits at the table it is reasonable to suppose that he reflects on his situation. Now that he receives so few commissions, he is in severe financial difficulties. But his financial crisis is secondary in his own mind to his doubts about the meaning of his work.

When he does paint, he does so with even greater mastery than previously. But his mastery has itself become a problem. Nobody before Hals painted portraits of greater dignity and greater sympathy, implying greater performance. But nobody before seized upon the

166

momentary personality of the sitter as Hals has done. It is with him that the notion of 'the speaking likeness' is born. Everything is sacrificed to the demands of the sitter's immediate presence.

Or almost everything, for the painter needs a defence against the threat of becoming the mere medium through whom the sitter presents himself. In Hals's portraits his brushmarks increasingly acquire a life of their own. By no means all of their energy is absorbed by their descriptive function. We are not only made acutely aware of the subject of the painting, but also of *how* it has been painted. With 'the speaking likeness' of the sitter is also born the notion of the virtuoso performance by the painter, the latter being the artist's protection against the former.

Yet it a protection that offers little consolation, for the virtuoso performance only satisfies the performer foɪ the duration of the performance. Whilst he is painting, it is as though the rendering of each face or hand by Hals is a colossal gamble for which all the sharp, rapid brushstrokes are the stakes. But when the painting is finished, what remains? The record of a passing personality and the record of a performance which is over. There are no real stakes. There are only careers. And with these — making a virtue of necessity — he has no truck.

Whilst he sits there, people — whose seventeenth-century Dutch costumes by now surprise us — come to the other end of the table and pause there. Some are friends, some are patrons. They ask to be painted. In most cases Hals declines. His lethargic manner is an aid. And perhaps his age as well. But there is also a certain defiance about his attitude. He makes it clear, that whatever may have happened when he was younger, he no longer shares their illusions.

Occasionally he agrees to paint a portrait. His method of

selection seems arbitrary: sometimes it is because the man is a friend; sometimes because the face interests him. (It must be made clear that this second act covers a period of several years.) When a face interests him, we perhaps gather from the conversation that it is because in some way or another the character of the sitter is related to the problem that preoccupies Hals, the problem of what it is that is changing so fundamentally during his lifetime.

It is in this spirit that he paints Descartes, that he paints the new, ineffective professor of theology, that he paints the minister Herman Langelius who "fought with the help of God's words, as with an iron sword, against atheism", that he paints the twin portraits of Alderman Geraerdts and his wife.

The wife in her canvas is standing, turned to the right and offering a rose in her outstretched hand. On her face is a compliant smile. The husband in his canvas is seated, one hand limply held up to receive the rose. His expression is simultaneously lascivious and appraising. He has no need to make the effort of any pretence. It is as though he is holding out his hand to take a bill of credit that is owing to him.

At the end of the second act a baker claims a debt of 200 florins from Hals. His property and his paintings are seized and he is declared bankrupt.

The third act is set in the old men's almshouse of Haarlem. It is the almshouse whose men and women governors Hals was commissioned to paint in 1664. The two resulting paintings are among the greatest he ever painted.

After he went bankrupt, Hals had to apply for municipal aid. For a long while it was thought that he was actually an inmate of the almshouse — which today is the Frans Hals Musuem — but apparently this was not the case. He experienced, however, both extreme poverty and the flavour of official charity.

In the centre of the stage the old men who are inmates sit at the same banqueting table, as featured in the First Act, with bowls of soup before them. Again it strikes us as a nineteenth-century scene — Dickensian. Behind the old men at the table, Hals, facing us, is between two canvases on easels. He is now in his eighties. Throughout the act he peers and paints on both canvases, totally without regard to what is going on elsewhere. He has become thinner as very old men can.

On the left on a raised platform are the men governors whom he is painting on one canvas; on the right, on a similar platform, are the women governors whom he is painting on the other canvas.

The inmates between each slow spoonful stare fixedly at us or at one of the two groups. Occasionally a quarrel breaks out between a pair of them.

The men governors discuss private and city business. But whenever they sense that they are being stared at, they stop talking and take up the positions in which Hals painted them, each lost in his own fantasy of morality, their hands fluttering like broken wings. Only the drunk with the large tilted hat goes on reminiscing and occasionally proposing a mock banquet toast. Once he tries to engage Hals in conversation.

(I should point out here that this is a theatrical image; in fact the governors and governesses posed singly for these group portraits.)

The women discuss the character of the inmates and offer explanations for their lack of enterprise or moral rectitude. When they sense that they are being stared at, the woman on the extreme right brings down her merciless hand on her thigh and this is a sign for the others to stare back at the old men eating their soup.

The hypocrisy of these women is not that they give while

feeling nothing, but that they never admit to the hate now lodged permanently under their black clothes. Each is secretly obsessed with her own hate. She puts out crumbs for it every morning of the endless winter until finally it is tame enough to tap on the glass of her bedroom window and wake her at dawn.

Darkness. Only the two paintings remain — two of the most severe indictments ever painted. They are projected side by side to fill a screen across the whole stage.

Offstage there is the sound of banqueting. Then a voice announces: He was eighty-four and he had lost his touch. He could no longer control his hands. The result is crude and, considering what he once was, pathetic.

1966.

Giacometti

The week after Giacometti's death *Paris-Match* published a remarkable photograph of him which had been taken nine months earlier. It shows him alone in the rain, crossing the street near his studio in Montparnasse. Although his arms are through the sleeves, his raincoat is hoicked up to cover his head. Invisibly, underneath the raincoat, his shoulders are hunched.

The immediate effect of the photograph, published when it was, depended upon it showing the image of a man curiously casual about his own well-being. A man with crumpled trousers and old shoes, ill-equipped for the rain. A man whose preoccupations took no note of the seasons.

But what makes the photograph remarkable is that it suggests more than that about Giacometti's character. The coat looks as though it has been borrowed. He looks as though underneath the coat he is wearing nothing except his trousers. He has the air of a survivor. But not in the tragic sense. He has become quite used to his position. I am tempted to say "like a monk", especially since the coat over his head suggests a cowl. But the simile is not accurate enough. He wore his symbolic poverty far more naturally than most monks.

Every artist's work changes when he dies. And finally no one remembers what his work was like when he was alive. Sometimes one can read what his contemporaries had to say about it. The difference of emphasis and interpretation is largely a question of historical development. But the death of the artist is also a dividing line.

It seems to me now that no artist's work could ever have been more changed by his death than Giacometti's. In twenty years no one will understand this change. His work will seem to have reverted to normal — although in fact it

171

will have become something different: it will have become
evidence from the past, instead of being, as it has been for
the last forty years, a possible preparation for something to
come.

The reason Giacometti's death seems to have changed his
work so radically is that his work had so much to do with an
awareness of death. It is as though his death confirms his
work: as though one could now arrange his works in a line
leading to his death, which would constitute far more than
the interruption or termination of that line — which would,
on the contrary, constitute the starting point for reading
back along that line, for appreciating his life's work.

You might argue that after all nobody ever believed that
Giacometti was immortal. His death could always be
deduced. Yet it is the fact which makes the difference. While
he was alive, his loneliness, his conviction that everybody
was unknowable, was no more than a chosen point of view
which implied a comment on the society he was living in.
Now by his death he has proved his point. Or — to put it a
better way, for he was not a man who was concerned with
argument — now his death has proved his point for him.

This may sound extreme, but despite the relative
traditionalism of his actual methods, Giacometti was a most
extreme artist. The neo-Dadaists and other so-called
iconoclasts of today are conventional window-dressers by
comparison.

The extreme proposition on which Giacometti based all
his mature work was that no reality — and he was concerned
with nothing else except the contemplation of reality —
could ever be shared. This is why he believed it impossible
for a work to be finished. This is why the content of any
work is not the nature of the figure or head portrayed but the
incomplete history of *his* staring at it. The act of looking was
like a form of prayer for him — it became a way of

approaching but never being able to grasp an absolute. It was the act of looking which kept him aware of being constantly suspended between being and the truth.

If he had been born in an earlier period, Giacometti would have been a religious artist. As it was, born in a period of profound and widespread alienation, he refused to escape through religion, which would have been an escape into the past. He was obstinately faithful to his own time, which must have seemed to him rather like his own skin: the sack into which he was born. In that sack he simply could not in all honesty overcome his conviction that he had always been and always would be totally alone.

To hold such a view of life requires a certain kind of temperament. It is beyond me to define that temperament precisely. It was visible in Giacometti's face. A kind of endurance lightened by cunning. If man was purely animal and not a social being, all old men would have this expression. One can glimpse something similar in Samuel Beckett's expression. Its antithesis was what you could see in Le Corbusier's face.

But it is by no means only a question of temperament: it is even more a question of the surrounding social reality. Nothing during Giacometti's lifetime broke through his isolation. Those whom he liked or loved were invited to share it temporarily with him. His basic situation — in the sack into which he was born — remained unchanged. (It is interesting that part of the legend about him tells of how almost nothing changed or was moved in his studio for the forty years he lived there. And during the last twenty years he continually recommenced the same five or six subjects.) Yet the nature of man as an essentially social being — although it is objectively proved by the very existence of language, science, culture — can only be felt subjectively through the experience of the force of change as a result of common action.

Insofar as Giacometti's view could not have been held during any preceding historical period, one can say that it reflects the social fragmentation and manic individualism of the late bourgeois intelligentsia. He was no longer even the artist in retreat. He was the artist who considered society as irrelevant. If it inherited his works it was by default.

But having said all this, the works remain and are unforgettable. His lucidity and total honesty about the consequences of his situation and outlook were such that he could still save and express a truth. It was an austere truth at the final limit of human interest; but his expressing of it transcends the social despair or cynicism which gave rise to it.

Giacometti's proposition that reality is unshareable is true in death. He was not morbidly concerned with the process of death: but he was exclusively concerned with the process of life as seen by a man whose own mortality supplied the only perspective in which he could trust. None of us is in a position to reject this perspective, even though simultaneously we may try to retain others.

I said that his work had been changed by his death. By dying he has emphasized and even clarified the content of his work. But the change — anyway as it seems to me at this moment — is more precise and specific than that.

Imagine one of the portrait heads confronting you as you stand and look. Or one of the nudes standing there to be inspected, hands at her side, touchable only through the thickness of two sacks — hers and yours — so that the question of nakedness does not arise and all talk of nakedness beco.nes as trivial as the talk of bourgeois women deciding what clothes to wear for a wedding: nakedness is a detail for an occasion that passes.

Imagine one of the sculptures. Thin, irreducible, still and

yet not rigid, impossible to dismiss, possible only to inspect, to stare at. If you stare, the figure stares back. This is also true of the most banal portrait. What is different now is how you become conscious of the track of your stare and hers: the narrow corridor of looking between you — perhaps this is like the track of a prayer if such a thing could be visualized. Either side of the corridor nothing counts. There is only one way to reach her — to stand still and stare. That is why she is so thin. All other possibilities and functions have been stripped away. Her entire reality is reduced to the fact of being seen.

When Giacometti was alive you were standing, as it were, in his place. You put yourself at the beginning of the track of his gaze and the figure reflected this gaze back to you like a mirror. Now that he is dead, or now that you know that he is dead, you take his place rather than put yourself in it. And then it seems that what first moves along the track comes from the figure. It stares, and you intercept the stare. Yet however far back you move along the narrow path, the gaze passes through you.

It appears now that Giacometti made these figures during his lifetime, for himself, as observers of his future absence, his death, his becoming unknowable.

1966

Rodin and Sexual Domination

"People say I think too much about women," said Rodin to
William Rothenstein. Pause. "Yet after all, what is there
more important to think about?"

The fiftieth anniversary of his death. Tens of thousands of
plates of Rodin sculptures have been specially printed this
year for anniversary books and magazine features. The
anniversary cult is a means of painlessly and superficially
informing a 'cultural *élite*' which for consumer-market
reasons needs constantly to be enlarged. It is a way of
consuming — as distinct from understanding — history.

Of the artists of the second half of the nineteenth century
who are today treated as masters, Rodin is the only one who
was internationally honoured and officially considered
illustrious during his working life. He was a traditionalist.
"The idea of progress," he said, "is society's worst form of
cant." From a modest *petit-bourgeois* Parisian family, he
became a *master* artist. At the height of his career he
employed ten other sculptors to carve the marbles for which
he was famous. From 1900 onwards his declared annual
income was in the region of 200,000 francs: in fact it was
probably considerably higher.

A visit to the Hôtel de Biron, the Rodin Museum in Paris,
where versions of most of his works are to be seen, is a
strange experience. The house is *peopled* by hundreds of
figures: it is like a Home or a Workhouse of statues. If you
approach a figure and, as it were, question it with your eyes,
you may discover much of incidental interest (the detail of a
hand, a mouth, the idea implied by the title, etc.). But, with
the exception of the studies for the Balzac monument and of
the *Walking Man* which, made twenty years earlier, was a
kind of prophetic study for the Balzac, there is not a single
figure which stands out and claims its own, according to the

first principle of free-standing sculpture: that is to say not a single figure which dominates the space around it.

All are prisoners within their contours. The effect on you is cumulative. You become aware of the terrible compression under which these figures exist. An invisible pressure inhibits and reduces every possible thrust outwards into some small surface event for the fingertips. "Sculpture," Rodin claimed, "is quite simply the art of depression and protuberance. There is no getting away from that." Certainly there is no getting away from it in the Hôtel de Biron. It is as though the figures were being forced back into their material: if the same pressure were further increased, the three-dimensional sculptures would become bas-reliefs: if increased yet further the bas-reliefs would become mere imprints on a wall. The *Gates of Hell* are a vast and enormously complex demonstration and expression of this pressure. *Hell* is the force which presses these figures back into the door. *The Thinker,* who overlooks the scene, is clenched against all outgoing contact: he shrinks from the very air that touches him.

During his lifetime Rodin was attacked by philistine critics for 'mutilating' his figures — hacking off arms, decapitating torsos, etc. The attacks were stupid and misdirected, but they were not entirely without foundation. Most of Rodin's figures have been reduced to less than they should be as independent sculptures: they have suffered oppression.

It is the same in his famous nude drawings in which he drew the woman's or dancer's outline without taking his eyes off the model, and afterwards filled it in with a water-colour wash. These drawings, though often striking, are like nothing so much as pressed leaves or flowers.

This failure of his figures (always with the exception of the *Balzac*) to create any spatial tension with their surroundings passed unnoticed by his contemporaries because they were preoccupied with their literary interpretations, which were sharpened by the obvious sexual significance of many of the sculptures. Later it was ignored because the revival of interest in Rodin (which began about fifteen to twenty years ago) concentrated upon the mastery of 'his touch' upon the sculptural surface. He was categorized as a sculptural 'Impressionist'. Nevertheless it is this failure, the existence of this terrible pressure upon Rodin's figures, which supplies the clue to their real (if negative) content.

The figure of the emaciated old woman, *She Who Was Once the Helmet-Maker's Beautiful Wife,* with her flattened breasts and her skin pressed against the bone, represents a paradigmatic choice of subject. Perhaps Rodin was dimly aware of his predisposition.

Often the action of a group or a figure is overtly concerned with some force of compression. Couples clasp each other (*vide The Kiss* where everything is limp except his hand and her arm both pulling inwards). Other couples fall on each other. Figures embrace the earth, swoon to the ground. A fallen caryatid still bears the stone that weighs her down. Women crouch as though pressed, hiding, into a corner.

In many of the marble carvings, figures and heads are meant to look as if they have only half emerged from the uncut block of stone: but in fact they look as though they are being compressed into and are merging with the block. If the implied process were to continue, they would not emerge independent and liberated: they would disappear.

Even when the action of the figure apparently belies the pressure being exerted upon it — as with certain of the smaller bronzes of dancers — one feels that the figure is still the malleable creature, unemancipated, of the sculptor's moulding hand. This hand fascinated Rodin. He depicted it holding an incomplete figure and a piece of earth and called

179

it *The Hand of God.*

Rodin explains himself:

"No good sculptor can model a human figure without dwelling on the mystery of life: this individual and that in fleeting variations only reminds him of the immanent type; he is led perpetually from the creature to the creator . . . That is why many of my figures have a hand, a foot, still imprisoned in the marble block; life is everywhere, but rarely indeed does it come to complete expression or the individual to perfect freedom." (Isadora Duncan, *My Life,* London, 1969.)

Yet if the compression which his figures suffer is to be explained as the expression of some kind of pantheistic fusion with nature, why is its effect so disastrous in sculptural terms?

Rodin was extraordinarily gifted and skilled as a sculptor. Given that his work exhibits a consistent and fundamental weakness, we must examine the structure of his personality rather than that of his opinions.

Rodin's insatiable sexual appetite was well-known during his lifetime, although since his death certain aspects of his life and work (including many hundreds of drawings) have been kept secret. All writers on Rodin's sculpture have noticed its sensuous or sexual character: but many of them treat this sexuality only as an ingredient. It seems to me that it was the prime motivation of his art — and not merely in the Freudian sense of a sublimation.

Isadora Duncan in her autobiography describes how Rodin tried to seduce her. Finally — and to her later regret — she resisted.

"Rodin was short, square, powerful with close-cropped head and plentiful beard . . . Sometimes he murmured the names of his statues, but one felt that names meant little to him. He ran his hands over them and caressed them. I remember thinking that beneath his hands the marble seemed to flow like molten lead. Finally he took a small quantity of clay and pressed it between his palms. He breathed hard as he did so . . . In a few moments he had formed a woman's breast . . . Then I stopped to explain to him my theories for a new dance, but soon I realised that he was not listening. He gazed at me with lowered lids, his eyes blazing, and then, with the same expression that he had before his works, he came towards me. He ran his hands over my hips, my bare legs and feet. He began to knead my whole body as if it were clay, while from him emanated heat that scorched and melted me. My whole desire was to yield to him my entire being . . .''

Rodin's success with women appears to have begun when he first began to become successful as a sculptor (aged about forty). It was then that his whole bearing — and his fame — offered a promise that Isadora Duncan describes so well because she describes it obliquely. His promise to women is that he will mould them: they will become clay in his hands. Their relation to him will become symbolically comparable to that of his sculptures.

"When Pygmalion returned home, he made straight for the statue of the girl he loved, leaned over the couch, and kissed her. She seemed warm: he laid his lips on hers again, and touched her breast with his hands — at his touch the ivory lost its hardness, and grew soft: his fingers made an imprint on the yielding surface, just as wax of Hymettus melts in the sun and, worked by men's fingers, is fashioned into many different shapes, and made fit for use by being used." (Ovid, *Metamorphoses*, Book X.)

181

What we may term the Pygmalion promise is perhaps a general element in male attraction for many women. When a specific and actual reference to a sculptor and his clay is at hand, its effect simply becomes more intense because it is more consciously recognizable.

What is remarkable in Rodin's case is that he himself appears to have found the Pygmalion promise attractive. I doubt whether his playing with the clay in front of Isadora Duncan was simply a ploy for her seduction: the ambivalence between clay and flesh also appealed to him. This is how he described the Venus de' Medici:

"Is it not marvellous? Confess that you did not expect to discover so much detail. Just look at the numberless undulations of the hollow which unites the body and the thigh . . . Notice all the voluptuous curvings of the hip . . . And now, here, the adorable dimples along the loins . . . It is truly flesh . . . You would think it moulded by caresses! You almost expect, when you touch this body, to find it warm."

If I am right, this amounts to a kind of inversion of the original myth and of the sexual archetype suggested by it. The original Pygmalion creates a statue with whom he falls in love. He prays that she may become alive so that she may be released from the ivory in which he has carved her, so that she may become independent, so that he can meet her *as an equal rather than as her creator*. Rodin, on the contrary, wants to perpetuate an ambivalence between the living and the created. What he is to women, he feels he must be to his sculptures. What he is to his sculptures, he wants to be to women.

Judith Cladel, his devoted biographer, describes Rodin working and making notes from the model.

"He leaned closer to the recumbent figure, and fearing lest the sound of his voice might disturb its loveliness, he whispered: 'Hold your mouth as though you were playing the flute. Again! Again!'

Then he wrote: 'The mouth, the luxurious protruding lips sensuously eloquent . . . Here the perfumed breath comes and goes like bees darting in and out of the hive . . .'

How happy he was during these hours of deep serenity, when he could enjoy the untroubled play of his faculties! A supreme ecstasy, for it had no end:

'What a joy is my ceaseless study of the human flower!

'How fortunate that in my profession I am able to love and also to speak of my love!' '' (Quoted by Denys Sutton, "Triumphant Satyr", London, *Country Life,* 1966.)

We can now begin to understand why his figures are unable to claim or dominate the space around them. They are physically compressed, imprisoned, forced back by the force of Rodin as dominator. Objectively speaking these works are expressions of his own freedom and imagination. But because clay and flesh are so ambivalently and fatally related in his mind, he is forced to treat them as though they were a challenge to his own authority and potency.

That is why he never himself worked in marble but only in clay and left it to his employees to carve in the more intractable medium. This is the only apt interpretation of his remark: ''The first thing God thought of when he created the world was modelling.'' This is the most logical explanation of why he found it necessary to keep in his studio at Meudon a kind of mortuary store of modelled hands, legs, feet, heads, arms, which he liked to play with by seeing whether he could add them to newly created bodies.

Why is the *Balzac* an exception? Our previous reasoning already suggests the answer. This is a sculpture of a man of enomous power striding across the world. Rodin considered it his masterpiece. All writers on Rodin are agreed that he also identified himself with Balzac. In one of the nude studies for it the sexual meaning is quite explicit: the right hand grips the erect penis. This is a monument to male potency. Frank Harris wrote of a later clothed version and what he says might apply to the finished one: "Under the old monastic robe with its empty sleeves, the man holds himself erect, the hands firmly grasping his virility and the head thrown back." This work was such a direct confirmation of Rodin's own sexual power that for once he was able to let it dominate him. Or, to put it another way — when he was working on the *Balzac*, the clay, probably for the only time in his life, seemed to him to be masculine.

The contradiction which flaws so much of Rodin's art and which becomes, as it were, its most profound and yet negative content, must have been in many ways a personal one. But it was also typical of an historical situation. Nothing reveals more vividly than Rodin's sculptures, if analysed in sufficient depth, the nature of bourgeois sexual morality in the second half of the nineteenth century.

On the one hand the hypocrisy, the guilt, which tends to make strong sexual desire — even if it can be nominally satisfied — febrile and phantasmagoric; on the other hand the fear of women escaping (as property) and the constant need to control them.

On the one hand Rodin who thinks that women are the most important thing in the world to think about; on the other hand the same man who curtly says: "In love all that counts is the act."

1967

Romaine Lorquet

Romaine Lorquet was born in Lyons about fifty years ago. Soon after the war she was in Paris, where she knew Brancusi, Giacometti and Etienne-Martin, each of whom recognised and encouraged her as an artist. More than twenty years ago she left Paris to live and work in relative isolation in the country.

There she has made many carvings. I use the word carvings instead of sculptures because the first word fits a little less easily into the contemporary art world. Scarcely ever has she tried to place her work in any kind of contemporary artistic or cultural context. There is nothing, I think, evasive in this decision. She has simply chosen to remain outside.

And it is outside — in both a general and precise sense — that I have seen most of her carvings. They are on a hillside around a peasant's house, in which she lives; some lie on the earth beneath the trees, others are nearly lost in the undergrowth. A few are made of wood, most are made of stone. Their height varies between 30 and 90 centimetres. Sometimes grasses or roots have grown through them. They are not on display.

Most man-made objects refer back to the event of their own making. Their presence depends upon the use of the past tense. *This house was built of stone.* These carvings hardly refer back at all to their own making. They look neither finished nor unfinished. Like a tree or a river, they appear to exist in a continuous present. Their apparent lack of history makes them look inevitable.

Speculatively I have tried to imagine them in a different context. In a museum gallery, or a city street, or an apartment. Because they insist so little upon their own making, they would then look like something found in

nature. If they were thought of as being hand-made, they would seem to belong to another period, in either the remote past or future.

Even on the earth, under the fruit trees, they challenge the demarcation line to which we are accustomed between nature and art. They deceive us into thinking that they are on the far side of that frontier. Perhaps they occupy the area which art left empty when it relinquished its magical function over nature. Some of the carvings are fully carved only on three sides: on the fourth, the stone has been left blank. This could suggest that in the carver's mind they were to be placed against a wall. Yet I doubt it. I think it far more likely that the fourth side was left uncarved so that the carving could remain "attached" to the nature from which it was only half-emerging.

Each of these carvings brings something forward towards the viewer. Yet they do not represent specific forms. They are not portraits of anything. Nor are they abstractions. The carver has not dug for forms in nature and cleaned and purified them in order to set them up as symbols. Lorquet's work has nothing in common with Classical decoration or with the modern sculptures of Arp, Miro, Max Bill, or Henry Moore.

What do these carvings bring forward?

Within nature, space is not something accorded from the outside; it is a condition of existence born from within. It is what has been, or will be, *grown into*. Space in nature is what the seed contains. Symmetry is the spatial law of growth, the law of *spacing*. Again, its code is not imposed from the outside but works from within. What the carvings bring forward from nature is such space and symmetry. Their forms obey the same laws of assembly as the fruit or leaves on a tree. They are assembled in such a way that they promise continuity — not the continuity of a logical series, but of growth.

Each carving is a "chain" of unions, of meetings, of events, "giving to" to and "receiving" each other so that their sum total is a single event. This much is of course true of any successful sculpture. One could say the same of Michelangelo's *Moses*. But with these carvings the single event they add up to, extends beyond themselves to include the whole landscape from grass below to mountains in the distance.

On those mountains are countless uncarved rocks and stones. I have studied some of them to see whether, by concentrating my attention on them, I can make them work in the same way as the carved ones. They remain inert, fixed in themselves. Far from their bringing anything forward, they withdraw deeper and deeper into the remote finished state of their own being. Their existence answers only its own question.

By contrast, the carvings invoke unity. They have something in common with Sumerian sculpture. In that very early art, the assemblage of parts also resembled the clustering of tangible forms in nature: berries, cones, fruit, organs of the body, animal or human, flowers, roots. Metaphor was still embedded in the physical unity of the world. For example, a mouth in a face was the variant of a hole in the earth, or a leaf was the variant of a hand. Metamorphosis was considered a constant possibility, and sculpture was a celebration of the common material from which everything was made.

As the division of labour increased, art, like every other discipline, began to differentiate more and more sharply. Idealisation was one of its forms of differentiation. Sculptors competed with one another to carve the perfect mouth, the mouth which was perfectly and only itself. The more they succeeded, the greater the distinction became between the mouth and hole in the earth. Everything was divided into its type. Every distinction and distance became measurable. And empty space was born. For four centuries the drama of most European sculpture has been created out of defiance in face of this empty space. Yet for these carvings there is no such thing as empty space. There is only space *within* a system, including the space which surrounds them. Francois

Jacob.

"The power of assembling, of producing increasingly complex structures, even of reproducing, belongs to the elements that constitute matter. From particles to man, there is a whole series of integrations, of levels, of discontinuities. But there is no breach either in the composition of objects or in the reactions that take place in them; no change in 'essence'."

The experience which informs these carvings is also the experience of our own bodies. They work like a mirror. Not a mirror which denies the interior by reflecting the surface, but the mirror of another's eyes. In their reflection of us, we find not an image of ourselves, but recognition of our physical being. Exceptionally, in moments of revelation, one can have a similar experience of being recognised in front of a tree, a corn field, a river. The carvings bring a little forward from nature the potential of this experience. Yet they can bring it so far and no further. They combine confidence with extreme restraint. Why must they be so reticent? Or, to ask the same question another way, why are they half abandoned on a hillside?

All art, which is based on a close observation of nature, eventually changes the way nature is seen. Either it confirms more strongly an already established way of seeing nature or it proposes a new way. Until recently a whole cultural process was involved; the artist observed nature: his work had a place in the culture of his time and that culture mediated between man and nature. In post-industrial societies this no longer happens. Their culture runs parallel to nature and is completely insulated from it. Anything which enters that culture has to sever its connections with nature. Even natural sights (views) have been reduced in consumption to commodities.

The sense of continuity once supplied by nature is now supplied by the means of communication and exchange — publicity, TV, newspapers, records, radio, shop-windows, auto-routes, package holidays, currencies, etc. These, barring catastrophes — either personal or global — form a mindless stream in which any material can be transmitted and made homogeneous — including art.

The rejection implicit in these carvings of the present *institution of art,* is therefore functional not cultural. The distinction is important. The cultural rejection of art — the anti-art movement, cultivated primitivism like Dubuffet's, auto-destructive art, etc. — are dependent on the art they reject and so lead back into the museum and the institution of art. Duchamp was not an iconoclast: he was a new type of curator.

The rejection of the carvings is functional because the culture within which they would have to operate is incapable of mediating between society and nature. And so they are forced to attempt to do this themselves. They begin from a very close observation of nature; and then, single-handed, they try to refer these observations, these insights, back to nature. Previously the referring-back would have been a gradual, indirect and socially mediated process. Here it becomes immediate, simple and physical, because the carvings have scarcely broken from nature. They refuse the *distinction* of art in our time.

Sometimes the vision of an individual imagination can outstrip the social forms of the existing culture — including the social form of art. When this happens the works produced by that imagination exist, not only in a personal but also in an historical solitude.

A butterfly alights on one of the carvings, closes its wings, becomes like the infinitely thin blade of an axe buried in the stone, opens and shuts its wings, flies off.

There is a paragraph by Marx which exists in the same solitude.

"The *human* essence of nature first exists only for *social* man; for only here does nature exist as the *foundation* of his own *human* existence. Only here has what is to him his *natural* existence become his *human* existence, and nature become man for him. Thus *society* is the unity of being of man with nature — the true resurrection of nature — the naturalism of man and the humanism of nature both brought to fulfillment." (Karl Marx: *Philosophical and Economic Manuscripts*)

1974

Field

Shelf of a field, green, within easy reach, the grass on it not yet high, papered with blue sky through which yellow has grown to make pure green, the surface colour of what the basin of the world contains, attendant field, shelf between sky and sea, fronted with a curtain of printed trees, friable at its edges, the corners of it rounded, answering the sun with heat, shelf on a wall through which from time to time a cuckoo is audible, shelf on which she keeps the invisible and intangible jars of her pleasure, field that I have always known, I am lying raised up on one elbow wondering whether in any direction I can see beyond where you stop. The wire around you is the horizon.

Remember what it was like to be sung to sleep. If you are fortunate, the memory will be more recent than childhood. The repeated lines of words and music are like paths. These paths are circular and the rings they make are linked together like those of a chain. You walk along these paths and are led by them in circles which lead from one to the other, further and further away. The field upon which you walk and upon which the chain is laid is the song.

Into the silence, which was also at times a roar, of my thoughts and questions forever returning to myself to search there for an explanation of my life and its purpose, into this concentrated tiny hub of dense silent noise, came the cackle of a hen from a nearby back garden, and at that moment that cackle, its distinct sharp-edged existence beneath a blue sky with white clouds, induced in me an intense awareness of freedom. The noise of the hen, which I could not even see, was an event (like a dog running or an artichoke flowering) in a field which until then had been awaiting a first event in

192

order to become itself realisable. I knew that in that field I could listen to all sounds, all music.

From the city centre there are two ways back to the satellite city in which I live: the main road with a lot of traffic, and a side road which goes over a level crossing . The second is quicker unless you have to wait for a train at the crossing. During the spring and early summer I invariably take the side road, and I find myself hoping that the level crossing will be shut. In the angle between the railway lines and the road there is field, surrounded on its other two sides by trees. The grass is tall in the field and in the evening when the sun is low, the green of the grass divides into light and dark grains of colour — as might happen to a bunch of parsley if lit up by the beam of a powerful lamp at night. Blackbirds hide in the grass and rise up from it. Their coming and going remains quite unaffected by the trains.

This field affords me considerable pleasure. Why then do I not sometimes walk there — it is quite near my flat — instead of relying on being stopped there by the closed level crossing? It is a question of contingencies overlapping. The events which take place in the field — two birds chasing one another, a cloud crossing the sun and changing the colour of the green — acquire a special significance because they occur during the minute or two during which I am obliged to wait. It is as though these minutes fill a certain area of time which exactly fits the spatial area of the field. Time and space conjoin.

The experience which I am attempting to describe by one tentative approach after another is very precise and is immediately recognizable. But it exists at a level of perception and feeling which is probably preverbal — hence, very much, the difficulty of writing about it.

Undoubtedly this experience must have a psychological history, beginning in infancy, which might be explained in psychoanalytical terms. But such explanations do not generalise the experience, they merely systematise it. The experience in one form or another is, I believe, a common one. It is seldom referred to only because it is nameless.

Let me now try to describe this experience diagrammatically in its ideal mode. What are the simplest things that can be said about it? The experience concerns a field. Not necessarily the same one. Any field, if perceived in a certain way, may offer it. But the *ideal* field, the field most likely to generate the experience, is:

1. A grass field. Why? It must be an area with boundaries which are visible — though not necessarily regular; it cannot be an unbounded segment of nature the limits to which are only set by the natural focus of your eyes. Yet within the area there should be a minimum of order, a minimum of planned events. Neither crops nor regularly planted lines of fruit trees are ideal.

2. A field on a hillside, seen either from above like a table top, or from below when the incline of the hill appears to tilt the field towards you — like music on a music stand. Again, why? Because then the effects of perspective are reduced to a minimum and the relation between what is distant and near is a more equal one.

3. Not a field in winter. Winter is a season of inaction when the range of what is likely to happen is reduced.

4. A field which is not hedged on all sides: ideally, therefore, a continental rather than an English field. A completely hedged field with only a couple of gates leading into it limits the number of possible exits or entrances (except for birds).

Two things might be suggested by the above prescriptions. The ideal field would apparently have certain qualities in common with (a) a painting — defined edges, an

accessible distance, and so on; and (b) a theatre-in-the-round stage — an attendant openness to events, with a maximum possibility for exits and entrances.

I believe, however, that suggestions like this are misleading, because they invoke a cultural context which, if it has anything whatsoever to do with the experience in question, can only refer *back* to it rather than precede it.

Given the ideal field now suggested, what are the further constitutive elements of the experience? It is here that the difficulties begin. You are before the field, although it seldom happens that your attention is drawn to the field before you have noticed an event within it. Usually the event draws your attention to the field, and, almost instantaneously, your own awareness of the field then gives a special significance to the event.

The first event — since every event is part of a process — invariably leads to other, or, more precisely, invariably leads you to observe others in the field. The first event may be almost anything, provided that it is not in itself over-dramatic.

If you saw a man cry out and fall down, the implications of the event would immediately break the self-sufficiency of the field. You would run into it from the outside. You would try to take him out of it. Even if no physical action is demanded, any over-dramatic event will have the same disadvantage.

If you saw a tree being struck by lightning, the dramatic force of the event would inevitably lead you to interpret it in terms which at that moment would seem larger than the field before you. So, the first event should not be over-dramatic but otherwise it can be almost anything:

Two horses grazing.

A dog running in narrowing circles.

An old woman looking for mushrooms.

A hawk hovering above.

Finches chasing each other from bush to bush.

Chickens pottering.

Two men talking.

A flock of sheep moving exceedingly slowly from one corner to the centre.

A voice calling.

A child walking.

The first event leads you to notice further events which may be consequences of the first, or which may be entirely unconnected with it except that they take place in the same field. Often the first event which fixes your attention is more obvious than the subsequent ones. Having noticed the dog, you notice a butterfly. Having noticed the horses, you hear a woodpecker and then see it fly across a corner of the field. You watch a child walking and when he has left the field deserted and eventless, you notice a cat jump down into it from the top of a wall.

By this time you are within the experience. Yet saying this implies narrative time and the essence of the experience is that it takes place outside such time. The experience does not enter into the narrative of your life — that narrative which, at one level or another of your consciousness, you are continually retelling and developing to yourself. On the contrary, this narrative is interrupted. The visible extension of the field in space displaces awareness of your own lived time. By what precise mechanism does it do this?

You relate the events which you have seen and are still seeing to the field. It is not only that the field frames them, it also *contains* them. The existence of the field is the precondition for their occurring in the way that they have done and for the way in which others are still occurring. All events exist as definable events by virtue of their relation to other events. You have defined the events you have seen primarily (but not necessarily exclusively) by relating them to the event of the field, which at the same time is literally and symbolically the *ground* of the events which are taking place within it.

You may complain that I have now suddenly changed my use of the word, ''event''. At first I referred to the field as a space awaiting events; now I refer to it as an event in itself. But this inconsistency parallels exactly the apparently illogical nature of the experience. Suddenly an experience of disinterested observation opens in its centre and gives birth to a happiness which is instantly recognisable as your own.

The field that you are standing before appears to have the same proportions as your own life.

1971

Picture Acknowledgements

ABOUT THE AUTHOR

John Berger, born in London in 1926, is well known as an art
critic, novelist, and film scriptwriter. His many books, inno-
vative in form and far-reaching in their historical and political insight, include *Ways of Seeing, Art and Revolution, The
Success and Failure of Picasso,* and the award-winning novel
G. His films with Alain Tanner include *La Salamandre* and
Jonah Will Be 25 in the Year 2000. Respected for his uncom-
promising judgements on art, Berger is one of Britain's most
influential art critics.

He lives at present in a small peasant community in France
which is the setting for his latest fiction, *Pig/Earth,* the first
part of a projected trilogy about the peasantry.